Acclaim for *Spontaneous Behavior*

Paul Austin has spent a lifetime as an actor, director, playwright, and teacher delving deeply into the act and art of theatre. This practical and well-crafted book is something only he could have written. It resonates with his passion for, curiosity about, and commitment to discovering how an actor can fulfill all of the potential inherent in their character and the play. To encourage actors in this demanding quest he first explores the primal sources of human behavior. He then offers a unique and comprehensive series of exercises to inspire actors toward meeting the exhilarating challenge of becoming "more of themselves by becoming somebody else."

—William Carden, Artistic Director,
Ensemble Studio Theatre, New York

Spontaneous Behavior is an actor's compendium, an exploration of the primal connections between performer and character; it's a trove of philosophy, method, and practice that delves into the primal needs of human behavior. Paul Austin's detailed examination of iconic stage characters like Chekhov's Masha, Williams's Tom Wingfield, Shakespeare's Hamlet and Gertrude, and other characters, reveals the effectiveness of his methods. The workbook lessons delve into the craft of acting. They provide a comprehensive way to practice body, mind, and feeling to help an actor develop and codify their approach to their task so that, within their own the neutral creative space, they will find common ground between themselves and the characters they are playing. If you are an experienced professional or new to this strange and enchanting endeavor, read on. You might discover a way that will allow you to always find your center, to create that quiet space.

—Zach Grenier, actor; Tony Award nominee,
33 Variations (Broadway); *Deadwood*;
Fight Club; The Good Fight (television)

Paul Austin has written a book like no other acting book. It's more than a detailed guide on how to build a character from text analysis to physical work on the body, gesture, and breathing. The approach to scenes is so vibrant and alive with possibilities for an actor that the exercises fly off the page. It's not only a valuable tool for audition, rehearsal, and performance, it's an exciting read that reawakens the wonder and mystery that is the art and craft of acting.

—James DeMarse, actor/writer; Drama Desk Award, *Orphans Home Cycle* (Off-Broadway); Artistic Director, 42nd St Workshop Theater

Both practical and inspiring, this book scintillates with respect for acting, and the integrity and unique persona of the actor. The exercises in the workbook section, have shown me how to accommodate any direction thrown my way, in whatever medium I happen to be working in.

—Karen Young, actor; *A Lie of the Mind* (Broadway); *Heading South* (film); *The Sopranos* (television)

Plundered from a lifetime of dedication to and love for the theater, Paul Austin has created a rigorous blueprint for delving into text, exploring and building character and craft, and creating the world of the play. *Spontaneous Behavior* is a guide to limitless artistic exploration, and is an invaluable tool for every committed actor, be they beginner, journeyman, or master craftsman.

—Julia Brothers, award-winning New York-based actor/writer; veteran of Broadway, regional theatre, standup comedy in NY and LA

SPONTANEOUS BEHAVIOR

The Art and Craft of Acting

Paul Austin

Also by Paul Austin:
Notes on Hard Times

ISBN: 978-1-7355762-6-8
Cover design and cover photograph: Alexis Siroc
Book design: Rowan Kehn

Turning Plow Press

For actors everywhere

Acknowledgments

I owe a special thanks to the hundreds of actors who have studied with me, trusting they have learned as much from me as I have from them.

For their contributions to this book, I am particularly indebted to Shirley Kaplan, for her initial encouragement, to Steve Garrison, for his suggestions on structure after the first draft, and to Rob Decina, for his creative and practical advice after every succeeding draft.

And a special acknowledgment to my wife and editor extraordinaire, Rilla Askew, for her unwavering belief and constant support.

Contents

Introduction   1

PART ONE
Feeling and Behavior

Chapter 1: A Definition of Feeling   6
Chapter 2: Passion as Ontological Source of Character   12
Chapter 3: Merging Life Passions   17
Chapter 4: Thought Process as Messenger
          to Emotional Behavior   22
Chapter 5: Emotional Behavior as Feeling in Action   34
Chapter 6: Inspiration   41

PART TWO
A Workbook for Creating Character

Introduction to the Workbook   48

Index of Exercises   52
1. The Power of Observation   53
2. Preparing the Actor's Body   58
3. Extreme Feeling   62
4. The Life Passion as Source of All Behavior   66
5. The Body Within   77
6. Instinctive Habits   87
7. Learned Habits   93
8. Sound and Speech   104
9. Breathing in Character   119
10. Place   126
11. Earning Choices   134
12. Shaping Performance   149

The Wrap   161

Introduction

Stage actors, except for actors who join a company where a formal way of working is developed to express a communal view of life, will spend most of their careers as vagabond players. They go from job to job challenged by a mandate to adapt their skills to the demands of each new collaboration. The reality of such working conditions means, for most actors, there is no one way to act.

I was fortunate to absorb this lesson when I was a young man studying at (then very small) Emerson College in Boston. I had two very different, very good acting teachers. One was Gertrude Binley Kay, known to us affectionately as "Maggie." She had been a Broadway actress in an era when American acting was still largely influenced by a declarative style popular during the Victorian Era. Now, she was a grand dame of eighty, full of life, energy, and a love of theatre with a capitol T. She taught mostly what was called the "presentational" approach to acting: stage presence and communicating to the audience. Our other teacher was Leo Nickole, a young man in his thirties, who had the passion and the knowledge to teach the Stanislavski approach.

Maggie was directing a fellow actor in rehearsal who was playing Valentine in *Love for Love*. Having worked with Leo to find the contradictions of love and lust in the character, the actor made his entrance as Valentine loaded with an unplayable ambiguity of feeling. Maggie stopped him. "Oh, no, dear. No, no, *no*. What are you doing?" He explained what he saw as the truth of his feelings. "Yes, yes. Very good, but we don't need to know all that. You are the leading part, my darling; you are a *star* and you must make an *entrance*. You must get our attention. You are here to *woo* her. All the rest of your lovely feelings will make themselves known when you try to woo her. So don't slouch in afraid of yourself. Take the stage and *woo* her." The scene came to life. With the Stanislavski approach, Leo had successfully illuminated the young actor to a greater and more complex range of feeling. But the actor was alive with so many feelings, his Valentine didn't know what to do with them. The thrill of feeling so much had distracted the actor from the feeling of the moment. In craft terms, he was trying to play text and subtext all at once. It was Maggie's instruction—that he need only play the action required by the play for all those "lovely feelings" to serve as a vibrant sub-text—which would make the single choice an act of spontaneous behavior rich with character. And as an eighteen-year-old freshman, I had witnessed two different approaches to acting complement each other.

A certain kind of dedication to the work is demanded from an actor whose professional life stutters between acceptance and rejection, job and no job, and the attendant fears and insecurities that intensify the usual distractions, despairs, losses of confidence, etcetera, of everyday life.

Stella Adler provided a clue to the kind of reward that inspires such dedication when she wrote: "Life beats down and crushes the soul and art reminds you that you have one."

If art *reminds* an actor of one's soul, then, as Adler's statement implies, the art itself is arguably a reflection of an actor's yearning to express it.

I would describe the soul of acting as *an indefinable sensation of wholeness experienced when feeling and behavior are in harmony as the expression of character.*

I first felt this sensation of wholeness at the age of seventeen, acting in a community theatre production of *Finian's Rainbow*. Somehow, on opening night, despite my innocent ignorance, I got a big laugh from the audience and, for the first time, I felt actually and completely *present*. From then on, it was a life in the theatre for me, and I went about learning how to act. Imagine that naïve, untutored young actor who found a life's vocation from a fortuitous audience response. Then fast forward and imagine him in Samuel Beckett's one-act masterpiece *Krapp's Last Tape*, after many years of study and work, calling on his craft to elongate the vowel in the word *spool*—a detail that allows him to give voice to an inexplicable urge to make sense of a life the character knows will come to an end before he can make peace with it.

I offer this example to illustrate how a passion for acting can often begin when a dormant intuitive instinct, which we may call inspiration, is awakened by an unforeseen providence. But, as Adler suggests, that intuitive inspiration runs the risk of being overwhelmed by life's demands. And that's when craft can come to the rescue.

Acting takes more than raw guts and chance, much as they are needed. Fine acting takes a surrender to vocation: a continual study of the practice of acting so that an actor can, as artist, maker of things, poet of flesh and spirit—at any time, in any circumstance—use any one or many of the acquired skills that make up an actor's craft and free inspiration from life's distractions.

In this sense, the partnership of inspiration and craft in the making of art may be the nearest we can define that elusive wonder we call "talent."

While *Spontaneous Behavior* is addressed primarily to stage actors, it also has value for actors who work in media and for performers in nearly all other forms of public expression: dance, music, mime, puppetry, standup comedy, storytelling, etcetera. It is also a useful source for all theatre persons who have made the art of the theatre their vocation, particularly directors, playwrights, and teachers, to enhance their collaborative skills for getting from page to stage.

In the book I've tried to give a sense of my way of working by using illustrations that show how different actors might work with specific characters. The book offers an approach to the art of acting meant to inspire each individual actor to follow Hamlet's advice and "hold the mirror" to a character at an angle that best reflects the actor's own view of human nature.

As a working actor and a teacher/coach dealing with actors in the present, in the flesh, I'm used to the luxury of time to say, re-say, adapt, improvise, critique, and encourage actors relative to their individual sensibilities. Such an approach necessarily uses language and tangential forays that apply to a specific actor or to a specific class of individual actors.

In my desire to reach as many actors as possible, I felt that a complete interpretation of one character by one actor would be counter-productive in that it would place too much emphasis on a specific interpretation at the expense of illustrating the many ways personal inspiration interacts with craft. To that end, I've chosen partial interpretations of well-known characters from classic, time-tested, widely available plays to show how different actors of differing sensibilities use the craft of acting.

Part One, on feeling and behavior, offers a close re-examination of the nature of feeling: how passion, thought process, and emotion combine to express a feeling that activates spontaneous character behavior.

Part Two, a Workbook, offers exercises and examples for creating a character faithful to both the uniqueness of an actor's interpretation and the collaborative process.

PART ONE

Feeling and Behavior

Chapter 1
A Definition of Feeling

When asked for a definition of acting, Noel Coward is reputed to have said that one had only to "learn the lines and stay out of the way of the furniture." It's not hard to imagine a cocktail party at which Sir Noel, a little impatiently but good-naturedly, used the line to fend off a slightly tipsy, and too earnest, devotee seeking advice for success from the great master. Amusing as it may have been under the influence of whiskey with a splash, Coward's clever remark coincidentally reflects an historical controversy over the role of emotion in the art of acting: whether an actor really feels emotion or merely simulates it—what Diderot called the paradox of acting.

Some, like Jean-Baptiste Coquelin, a French actor of the nineteenth century, believed that actors shouldn't feel emotion for itself but merely simulate emotion to allow the audience to experience it. Others, including Stanislavski—the most influential voice on acting of the twentieth century—believed that an actor couldn't be truthful without genuine emotion.

I view Diderot's paradox not as an either/or proposition but rather as a semantic confusion illustrated by how often we use the words *emotion* and *feeling* synonymously. For an actor, emotion and feeling are not identical. Feeling is not emotion, but emotion is part of feeling. True, they are almost as alike as twins, but a close look at what we might call the chemistry of feeling reveals they are related sequentially rather than simultaneously.

I'll take my cue from the second definition of emotion in the Oxford: "a moving out, migration, transference from one place to another." I'll speak of *emotional behavior,* rather than emotion, because emotional behavior more accurately describes the *expression of feeling in action.*

This book holds to the idea that, because of the self-evident truth that one cannot *not* feel, it's best to train the instrument to be capable of feeling what the character feels. Simply put, let's begin not by training ourselves to *indicate* feeling but by training ourselves to *share* feeling, because, while it sometimes can be stylistically valid for an actor to instruct an audience to feel, it's only when actor and audience *share* feeling that they cease to become each to other and enjoy that animated transcendence of being *us* which is the special providence of performing art.

The chemistry of feeling. Feeling can be defined as three sequential events happening in a time too quick to measure. The first is a *passionate response*—an overwhelming, utterly singular reaction to a stimulus. That passion then urges the mind to create a *thought process* to facilitate *emotional behavior* that will act out an intention to satisfy a need inherent in the passionate response.

Consider, for example, an actor playing Masha in a regional theatre in Cincinnati. Imagine Vershinin kisses her hand in the scene when he confesses his love. Imagine how that kiss stimulates a rush of love in the actor playing Masha. Imagine, then, that the passion of that love generates a thought process, which fills Masha with rapturous images of dancing the night away in a Moscow ballroom with one dashing young officer after another. The mental activity then transforms the passion into the emotional behavior of the moment, which the actor experiences in the scene as a mix of womanly desire and a girlish coyness that expresses itself with a slightly naughty dance by candlelight at two o'clock in the morning.

This, we could say, is a fulfilled feeling because it is the result of the sequential, active chemistry of passion, thought process, and the emotional behavior which satisfies an inherent need in the passion that prompted it. The upshot of the interior activity of these three properties—a passion of blood, a thought process of the mind, and the emotional behavior of the heart and mind, all three distinct but not separate from each other—is a spontaneous feeling. This spontaneous feeling triggers a series of spontaneous feelings in reaction to one another, the accumulation of which reveals character through spontaneous emotional behavior.

The essential substance of characterization is to embody the accumulated passions of a character's life.

The casual and the natural. Emotional behavior without passion as its source lacks genuine energy and suspense. Fear of unruly passions causes much of off-stage life to be spent distorting, disregarding, disguising, and denying passions, which results in a general, everyday habit of repressing passion because its subsequent behavior carries a burden of responsibility not always possible to satisfy.

On stage, actors will sometimes justify this seeming lack of passionate energy as being "natural." This frequently leads to the mistake of equating the casual with the natural—a confusion which leads to a negative kind of underplaying.

It's true enough that the portrayal of casual habits is essential to create the appearance of a character's everyday behavior. But plays are out to capture more than the verisimilitude of the casual. They're out to make trouble for characters. They create crises to force characters to reveal themselves.

Consider Simon Hench in Simon Grey's play *Otherwise Engaged* as an example of how to underplay in casual behavior a feeling still motivated by its essential passion.

Hench, as the playwright imagines him, has made a conscious choice as a matter of habit not to reveal his emotions. When his wife announces she is leaving him, he refuses to engage her in making a scene and tells her he doesn't see the point. Here we have a character that non-actors could, with justification, describe as unemotional. But appropriate as it may be to describe his outward behavior as unemotional, it is not accurate to describe him as unfeeling. He is *behaving* unemotionally because, in response to his wife's attempt to engage him, he suffers a passion to protect himself from his own cruelties and vulnerabilities. To affect his intention, Hench thinks of a person he dislikes who talks too much, which prompts him to tell his wife—with a dry, unemotional wit—why he'd rather not contribute to "this zestfully over-explicatory age."

So, even though the conscious behavior of the moment is unemotional in its outward appearance, the full life of the moment is not without feeling.

Watch Hench in the next moment after his wife leaves, hurt and angry. Watch him put on his headphones and listen, at high volume, to Wagner's *Parsifal* to allow himself the emotions he would not permit a moment earlier.

This striking moment is spontaneous because Hench's passion to protect himself is ever-present in the *feeling subtext* of the unemotional behavior in the previous moment.

A character, then, can seem unemotional in outward behavior while enduring a storm of emotion within because there is no such thing as not having feeling.

Feeling as raw material. We experience the richness of life through our natural and compulsive ability to feel. We talk about liking or disliking the "feel" of someone or something, of getting the "feel" of a situation. We even talk of getting the "feel" of an idea. There isn't anything that doesn't have a "feel" to it. Feeling is what captures and conveys the otherwise incomprehensible.

For the artist, the raw material of feeling can be found everywhere—in people, in places, in objects, in history itself. Merce Cunningham would sit motionless on a chair in a studio for hours and wait for the feel of the space to tell him how to move. John Cage would wait to be prompted into composition by the feel of a given silence. Jackson Pollock would demand that the feel of one dripped pattern show him another. Virginia Woolf shuddered to hear the rattle of death in the cold stone walls of a badly heated girls college. The full moon inspired the tragic spirit in Duse's portrayal of Mrs. Alving.

Can these inspirations be only the subconscious projections of the artist? I'd say, rather, that they are the result of the artist tuning into his raw material as Faulkner was tuned to his "little postage stamp of native soil" in Mississippi. Maya Lin's Vietnam War Memorial, for instance, was inspired not only by the privacies of her own feeling about the war but by the feel of the stone itself and by finding a location that had the right feel for the monument. A feeling can also be thought of as a state of being or, as I prefer for acting purposes, a *feeling condition*.

The question is not whether an actor *is* feeling, but how an actor *uses* feeling. It is how feeling is *expressed*—that is to say, emotional behavior—which defines a character. The rush of love that Masha feels when Vershinin kisses her hand is her passion for life, and the near simultaneous impulse she feels to waltz around the room to a remembered Tchaikovsky tune expresses in behavior the character of her life's passion.

Getting hold of this natural process is tricky in that it happens in a time too quick to measure. Bat an eyelash, bite a lip, tug an ear, and we are on to the next moment. The chemistry of spontaneous feeling is so condensed as to be combustible with suspense. Any moment now, anything might happen: Lear with "hideous rashness" might do something other than deny Cordelia. Oedipus might do other than blind himself upon learning he committed patricide. Estragon may decide not to wait for Godot. Who knows what Masha might do the moment she realizes Vershinin is lost to her?

The actor playing Masha goes on to the next moment because her fulfilled feeling is pregnant with possible actions. In that split-second stillness of the present, her feeling has recorded the past and is preparing to launch the future.

Next, I'll look at *passion, thought process,* and *emotional behavior* in more detail and with illustrations.

The next chapter deals with how the unconscious passion to survive is the fundamental source of emotional behavior.

Chapter 2
Passion as Ontological Source of Character

Think for a moment of the actor's billing on the program:

Georgina Doe............................ Masha
and as it often appears on the bio page:
Georgina Doe (Masha)

On the face of it, being two persons at the same time would seem an impossibility. Yet this seeming impossibility becomes a reality because a playgoer looking at the billing page is *predisposed to believe* that actor and character are one. Shakespeare recognized this state of readiness in the prologue to *Henry V,* when the Chorus appeals for playgoers to put their "imaginary forces" to work and "piece out (the) imperfections" of the play to make real the battle of Agincourt on an empty stage.

To achieve the easier-said-than-done magical feat of two people existing as one charismatic presence, an actor needs to embody four persons simultaneously: the actor's own conscious and unconscious selves, and the character's conscious and unconscious selves. In what we might call a quadrangle of known and unknown selves, or the geometry of character, an actor merges a whole, dual self with a character's whole, dual self.

This is a whole unknowable, finally, to both actor and character, because what is unknown is unavailable in a literal sense to either character or actor. Nevertheless, what's unknown is a *felt reality* in the *merged presence* of actor and character. To achieve the felt reality of that presence, we'll need to fashion a craft that intuits the unknown as a working partner of the known.

The purpose of this chapter is to find the passionate need, the ontological source, that predisposes both actor and playgoer to believe this extraordinary collaboration is possible. To find the source of this predisposition, let's start with the playgoer and then track it back to the actor.

One of the more useful enjoyments of the theatre is its function as a ritual rehearsal of human crisis. And it does so because it reinvigorates our neglected passions—a pleasure akin to Aristotle's tragic exhilaration.

Imagine, if you will, the theatre is full as the house lights go to half, signaling the time for playgoers to prepare for a journey into another reality.

A moment or two later, the house lights fade to black. Now imagine in that time within time before the first light of the play, no matter what they may be consciously thinking, each playgoer can feel themselves in the dark of a prehistoric no-man's-land in which anything is possible. Then imagine they experience their predisposition to believe as a feeling pulsing with excitement and expectation as they wait to be transported from their everyday reality to where they know not, for reasons they've yet to discover.

When light dawns on stage, the artistry of sets, lights, sound, spoken word, sometimes the reputations of stars and playwrights, and the habit of playgoing, will arouse a playgoer's predisposition to believe in the magical present of a certain time and place in the history of human civilization. But these production elements, however well executed, are not enough to gain the playgoer's full consent to believe. For that, we need the actor.

A play becomes a reality in live performance when a playgoer *consents* to *believe* actor and character are one and the same person. Only a human being in the physical presence of an actor "in character" can guarantee the playgoer's consent.

The ontological passion that makes actor as character possible and brings the playgoer along into the full reality of the play is what we're after.

The source. There are two instinctive passions, nearly simultaneously embedded in genetic code, that provide the source for all behavior.

All human lives first suffer from the pain and danger of being pushed and pulled from the comfort of the womb into a cold and hostile atmosphere. The newborn infant instinctively calls on a passion that activates a search for warmth and sustenance to survive the suffering of a strange new world. Thus, every feeling response is first a dual bio-neurological response of interplay between a passion of suffering and a passion to act to ease the suffering.

As I have used *instinct* and *passion* in the above example, the two words may seem to be synonymous. In fact, they are not. To better understand how this dual embryonic response relates to acting, recall that, in Chapter 1, we distinguished passion from thought process so that an actor could work in the time-within-time it takes to create emotional behavior. So, too, we can make a similar distinction between passion and instinct to facilitate finding the source of spontaneous behavior.

It all starts when the brain instinctively releases chemicals from the adrenal gland to warn the body it is suffering a passionate *reaction,* which, in an immeasurable but distinct time, the brain prompts another instinct in the mind to take a passionate *action.* In other words, the brain affects the body before the mind recognizes what to do with it.

This dual responsive interplay between a passion of suffering and a passion to survive is the ontological source of all spontaneous behavior. Furthermore, because it is the first to occur instinctively, a passion of suffering is the single root source of spontaneous behavior.

All persons, therefore, are motivated to carve out a life for themselves in response to a universal, ontological life passion to survive human suffering.

As we mature, our passions of suffering change according to life circumstances. Each different passion of suffering begets a different passion for an act of survival. These are our learned passions. Thus, the character of our lives is a series of learned passions, some of which become ingrained habit over time

The way it works. The first definition of passion in the Oxford English Dictionary draws on the Christian idea that the life of Jesus can be regarded as the *passion of his suffering*. This, in effect, is an act of religious faith on the part of the believer. So it is, too, in the theatre. Actors often refer to the tragic passion of Blanche Dubois or the comic passion of Malvolio.

Many, including myself, believe an actor creates a character by an act of poetic faith, a notion famously described by Samuel Taylor Coleridge in the making of a poem. Coleridge's ambition was to "…transfer from our inward nature a human interest and a semblance of truth sufficient to procure for these shadows of imagination that willing suspension of disbelief for the moment, which constitutes poetic faith."

A character is an actor's poem, the "semblance of truth" made from the "shadows of imagination."

The second definition of passion in the Oxford defines it as "the fact or condition of being acted upon or affected by external agency; subjection to external force." As good a template as any for how an actor uses Coleridge's willing suspension of disbelief to gain the poetic faith that transports the work of art called a character from page to stage.

First, an actor turns Coleridge's willing suspension of *disbelief* to the more active need *to believe* as an act of poetic faith in the life passion to survive the external force that causes the passion of human suffering. Now think of the character as the external agent for putting that faith to work.

For example: One of the greatest of American literary and dramatic achievements is the group of ten plays August Wilson wrote for what's called the American Century Cycle. Wilson's life passion to write out of his own passion for human dignity evolved into a life passion for human dignity in Troy Maxson, the embittered father in *Fences.* An actor's life passion to act evolves into Troy's life passion. Thus, a work of theatre art is made singular and universal because author, actor, and playgoer unite their life passions to survive human suffering in the living presence of Troy Maxson's life passion for human dignity.

Next: how actor and character merge life passions.

Chapter 3
Merging Life Passions

Something went wrong for the actor playing Hamlet at today's rehearsal as they rehearsed Act III, Scene 4, the closet scene. He began to feel strangely displaced, almost as though he could hear someone else saying the lines. He could see that the actor playing Gertrude was not reacting to Hamlet. She was worried about *him* not Hamlet! So much so that, after the scene, she quietly asked him, "Are you all right?"

When the director, equally frustrated, calls for tomorrow's rehearsal to begin with the closet scene again, the actor finds himself thinking about whether he should quit or wait until he gets fired.

As he leaves rehearsal he intends to go straight home, but when he comes up out of the subway, he finds he doesn't want to be alone. Rather than inflict his roiled self on anyone he knows, he goes into a bar across the street to have a beer, hoping to be anonymous in the company of strangers while he pulls himself together.

He tries listening to the piped in music of a popular FM station and observing the other people in the bar. But he can't keep his mind off his troubles. *Damn Hamlet anyway. That's all you ever hear about. Greatest part ever written. You haven't acted unless you've played Hamlet. Well, that's it. I've had enough. I don't want the trouble, give the part to my understudy. He's a better actor than me—what? Did I just say I DON'T LIKE HAMLET? That's not possible. How can you not like Hamlet? I'm crazy. That's it. I've gone off my rocker, that's why I can't act.*

He takes a long swig.

But God damn it! I was ON it! I mean, I was on fire with it!

He remembers how at the audition he'd known his interpretation worked—for him and for the play. How he'd seen Hamlet as a prince whose right to the throne had been usurped by his uncle, Claudius, and was convinced his mother's marriage was part of a plot. "Frailty thy name is woman" he'd ascribed to a hidden self in Gertrude, released by erotic obsession, sick with lust for intrigue and conspiracy: a self that had only pretended to love his father. She and Claudius had stolen the throne! A throne that would have been rightfully his! He would play Hamlet as surprised and thrilled by an unexpected lust to wear the crown—a newborn passion so fierce as to motivate a revenge that would make all of Hamlet's seeming hesitations no more than disguises to hide his true ambition.

The actor's spirits almost lift as he remembers how he'd auditioned the "too, too solid flesh" soliloquy not as a mournful contemplation of suicide but as a grateful release of his rage at having been betrayed. He'd begun the speech wishing not for his own suicide but for his mother to kill herself. And he'd been cast in the part because his audition so coincided with the director's vision for the play.

I killed them at the first readthrough, he thinks, *I was in charge, I drove the play! I was fierce, I was dangerous! They couldn't keep their eyes off me! What the hell went wrong?*

He can't help but imagine the people in the bar seeing him in today's lousy rehearsal. He leaves his beer unfinished and walks the two blocks home.

In his apartment he does twenty push-ups and twenty sit-ups before he makes himself a cup of coffee. He vows that if he can't give the audience a real Hamlet, he can, at least, entertain them with some genuine swordplay. The physical exercise makes him feel confident enough to look at the text again.

He scans the "O what a rogue" soliloquy in Act II, Scene 2, but nothing happens. Words, words. He doesn't feel a thing. A panic takes hold. He dreads tomorrow's rehearsal.

He goes back to the closet scene, hoping for a clue that will bring some life to it. He feels guilty for having played the scene so boringly as to ruin what would have been a good day for the actor playing Gertrude. At the very least, he wants to respect his fellow actor by finding something honest, something to offer her, when they work the scene tomorrow.

Rereading the scene, he sees he wasn't that bad for the whole scene. It was only in the very last beat that he'd lost feeling: when his Hamlet asked his mother to throw away the worser part of her heart and live with the better half by refraining from going to bed with his father's brother. The words that should have been said with a fury that reflected his interpretation had, seemingly for no reason, lost all meaning for him. He'd compensated by underplaying the next sixteen lines so badly that when the actor playing Gertrude, not three feet away from him, gave him a look of concern and tugged an ear toward him, he realized she could hardly hear him. That inappropriate choice forced its way out later as a luridly overacted explosion of self-pity with "…but heaven hath pleased it so / To punish me with this and this with me." In short, for underplaying badly in one place, the actor was compelled to overplay badly in another. So. Problem found. He'd been okay until that one beat. Next question: why?

In the closet scene in Act III, he'd interpreted Gertrude's unwillingness to look at the portrait of his father as proof of her wickedness. He'd made that choice because he's taken his father's ghost's admonition to "leave her to heaven / And to those thorns that in her bosom lodge…" as his justification to punish her. Given the scene in Act III is urged on by the voice of his father's ghost, he makes a guess that the clue to what went wrong might lay in the scene with the ghost in Act I.

When he rereads the scene, he realizes he was so intent on his desire for revenge, he hadn't responded to how his fellow actor played Hamlet's father's ghost. Now he remembers how the actor's eyes were wet with love and compassion when he spoke of the pain his wife, his queen, Hamlet's mother, would suffer in eternity.

As he takes the last sip of coffee, the actor is embarrassed to realize he made a fundamental acting mistake—something he was supposed to have learned not to do in his first scene study class: he'd heard his father's ghost speak as he'd *wanted* to hear him and not as his fellow actor had *actually* spoken. That's how he came to misread Hamlet's change of intention in the later scene with his mother.

Next day in rehearsal he looks at his mother with his father's eyes and is nearly torn in two by the surge of love he feels ripping through his fury for revenge. All the word stresses he'd used throughout the scene yesterday, to indicate feelings he hadn't felt, have disappeared. And when, toward the end of the scene, he says, "I must be cruel, only to be kind," he experiences a new feeling so strangely beautiful as to be unnamable—a feeling that so moves the actor playing Gertrude, she gives him a hug after they finish the scene.

Why, then, did the actor lose all feeling in the previous rehearsal with a choice he thought appropriate to Hamlet's passion for revenge? If the actor believes his mother conspired in the murder of his father to deprive him of his rightful crown, why say he misread the intention of that one beat in the scene? If the actor is entitled to his interpretation, couldn't the fault lie other than in his interpretation? Couldn't he have simply missed the moment for no discernible reason except the usual distractions that happen in every rehearsal? Why did the choice for Hamlet to love his mother work for him and not the choice to punish her?

As I noted in the previous chapter, the play is a crossroads where the passions of both actor and character converge, and an actor's passion is the determining factor in individual characterization.

The actor's first engagement with Hamlet's passion for revenge was met with his passion to be an artist with an interpretation unique to himself. In the one beat of the closet scene, the flash of feeling in the moment was, once again, mistakenly motivated by a *thought process* prompted by the actor's passion for an original interpretation. He had tried, without success, to urge Hamlet to punish his mother because he was blind to Hamlet's *contradictory passion* to save his mother's soul.

In other words, he was thinking for himself and not for Hamlet. The beat played badly because, in that flash of feeling which caused Hamlet to force his mother to look at the portrait of his father, he was thinking *stay on it, keep the fire going,* forcing an interpretive choice on the scene. But when he changed his thoughts to *see him, mother, please see my father, save your soul,* the scene played spontaneously: clear proof it was a choice he hadn't realized he *wanted* to make. It's a choice that in no way betrayed the actor's interpretation but rather added nuance to the characterization and, in fact, enhanced his interpretation because Hamlet's weakening to save his mother's soul provides an obstacle for the actor/character to overcome in order to earn his passion for the crown.

In this chapter, I've limited our investigation to how one particular actor uses thought process to merge his life passion with the character's. But what's true for one actor playing Hamlet may not be so for another. The permutations of interpretation are as varied as there are numbers of actors. The fact is, every actor brings a trunkful of a lifetime's psychological habits—cultural, social, and a host of intangible influences—to the creation of character, all of which are crucial to an original interpretation because they charge the actor with unique mental activities.

For that reason, the following chapter uses different actors playing different parts to illustrate how to master thinking in character.

Chapter 4
Thought Process as Messenger to Emotional Behavior

There's not much of human endeavor that can rival the force of energy experienced by an actor as Lady Macbeth, in the flesh, in the moment of the raven's hoarse cry, as she chooses to transcend gender and conscience in order to effect the murder of Duncan. It's the potency of her *thought*—her near simultaneous mental calculations of the witches' prophecy, the success of Macbeth in the battlefield, and the fortuitous arrival of Duncan—which *organizes her passion* for power and spurs her *emotional* appeal to those eerie "murdering ministers" to unsex her and fill her "from the crown to the toe top-full of direst cruelty."

This ability is made possible not by the size of the actor's word dictionary but by the mental rigor, verbal and otherwise, which allows her to *think in character*: that is, to discover an appropriate thought that transforms the passion of a moment into an emotional expression of feeling behavior, made elegant with personal style because it is exquisite with resonances common to both actor and character.

Because feeling behavior that proceeds from a passionate response happens in a time-within-time too quick to measure, thought process and emotional behavior would seem to be simultaneous. But thought is quite distinct from emotional behavior. It is a bio-neurological activity of the brain that results in a process of mind which functions as a messenger to instruct us how to generate emotional behavior from a passionate response.

Thought as word and sensory experience. Consider Romeo slipping through the dark, dangerous streets of Verona in search of a forbidden love. Consider the flashes of joy, terror, anger, and longing that course through him in the black shadows of a moonlit night as he leaps over the forbidden boundary of the Capulets' wall. Imagine then the rush of passion he must experience upon seeing the light in Juliet's window. What a birth of unutterably endless possibilities must be inspired in his young heart! And what extraordinary activity must be going on in his mind! "But soft!" says he, so as to give his synapses time to fire, "what light through yonder window breaks?" And from all the memories, sensations, and imaginings flashing through his brain, his mind creates, in an instant, a metaphor—that most wondrous human ability to apprehend meaning beyond logic. "It is the east," Romeo says, as he feels the power of a love which can turn night into day, "and Juliet is the sun."

Words alone, though often used successfully as metaphor—as when Romeo sees Juliet as the sun—are not always enough to express this potentially endless mental activity. Fortunately, the human mind is not restricted to using language alone for metaphor. The mind is also in the business of translating the body's senses into metaphors for the otherwise unsayable. Because we see in color, we say we're feeling blue or feeling red with fury. The actor we met playing Masha in a regional theatre production of *Three Sisters* can hum the sounds of Tchaikovsky to express a longing she can't put into words. Helene Weigel, playing Mother Courage hearing the news of her son's death, can black out in her mind and drop to the floor in a metaphorical faint.

Imagine how one smell can exceed the parameters of the conscious mind as it releases a multitude of memories in one moment, and then consider all the other senses with their attendant cultural, psychological, primitive, collective, and individual memories combined with improvisations, dreams, and visions, multiplied by a thousand, and one begins to get an idea of the extraordinary mental activity inspired by one moment of passion.

It is barely short a miracle to structure a thought process from this bewilderment of riches, sparked by human senses, that sets emotional behavior into action.

Thinking in character. When actors aren't doing well, they're often accused of thinking too much, of being too "intellectual." Since it's patently absurd that anyone could be thinking too much, the simpler truth can only be the actor is *not* thinking in character.

Actors have differences with characters for the obvious reason that actors are different people than the characters they play. Sometimes those differences are major, sometimes minor, sometimes appropriate, sometimes not.

Recall that behavior is born of feeling, and feeling is an instantaneous sequence of passion, thought process, and emotional behavior. One feeling creates a response which motivates another feeling, and so on, each successive feeling having its own unique blend of passion, thought process, and emotional behavior. As we saw with the actor playing Hamlet, thinking in character is the linchpin that holds together all the nuances of interpretation throughout performance. And when all the actors in a company are thinking in character, you have a unique interpretation of the play.

Appropriate and inappropriate thoughts. An actor's personal thoughts will sometimes slip into the fictional life of the play, as they are bound to do in the natural trial and error of rehearsals. Thinking one's personal thoughts will affect the character's emotional behavior and can often make the choice of behavior seem "wrong" for the desired interpretation.

I put "wrong" in quotes because I prefer "appropriate" or "inappropriate" rather than "right" or "wrong" to describe choices. To my mind, so-called mistakes—even when inappropriate to interpretation—are better thought of as tangential journeys to discover appropriate choices for character behavior.

We first saw the actor playing Hamlet lose spontaneity because an inappropriate choice came from his personal ambition. We also saw how a tangential journey in search of an appropriate choice to think in character made for a rich variation of behavior in the scene.

Two actors, many choices. Let's compare the different ways the actor playing Hamlet and another actor might make different choices for the same moment in Act I, scene 4, Hamlet's first meeting with Claudius.

First, imagine how two actors can play the same choice from *two different life passions.*

Our actor, upon hearing Claudius say, "But now my cousin Hamlet, and my son," might experience a passionate rage. Another actor might entertain a passionate grief. Though both actors are motivated by different life passions, they could both render the aside "a little more than kin and less than kind" with a similar ironic bitterness. The interpretive choice of emotional behavior would seem alike but remain unique to each actor because it is motivated by two different passions put into play by two different thought processes. The second actor suffering grief might recall his father as a king loved by his people. Our actor suffering rage might fasten his attention on his mother's rumpled "incestuous sheets."

The two passions thus carry two different subtextual nuances of tone into the playing of the moment. You might say that each actor has imprinted his version of ironic bitterness on their respective passions of grief and rage.

Now, take a look at what happens when the two actors carry in the *same passion of grief* in Hamlet's response, and how each uses a different thought process to arrive at a different interpretation of the moment:

Our actor might smell the damp sheets of his mother's lust and choke with disgust on the line; the other might hear the cries from his father's grave and whisper a sob into the line. In this instance, the emotional behavior of the moment is boldly different from one actor to another, even though the passion of the moment is the same for both actors.

Assuming, in this instance, both choices are interpretively acceptable for both actors in their respective productions, each actor, then, has used a different thought process to create an emphasis of emotional behavior to serve his respective interpretation.

More than one appropriate choice. If two actors can have two different appropriate choices for a moment, so too can one actor have more than one appropriate choice.

Suppose an actor playing Juliet catches a twinkle of rebellion in the eyes of Romeo when she asks him to deny his father and refuse his Montague name. Now suppose this twinkle in Romeo's eyes prompts Juliet's mind to have a thought-picture of a little girl chasing a butterfly in a meadow, and the little girl in her mind's eye leads her to jump up and down like an excited schoolgirl at a rock concert when she finds the words to say, "Or, if thou wilt not, be but sworn my love / And I'll no longer be a Capulet." Suppose further that, after rehearsal, the actor playing Romeo tells her how wonderful the moment had been.

So far, so good. Things are going well. As a musician might say, the two actors are "cooking."

Now, look at what happens at the next rehearsal when the actor's thought process comes, inadvertently, from an inappropriate need. Suppose the actor playing Juliet is affected for the first time by a less well-lit part of the rehearsal stage that calls to mind the night shadows of the actual scene. Imagine the unexpected darkness causes her a moment's fear. Now suppose this unforeseen change causes the actor to think in a flash, *Oh my God, this can't be right. This isn't what I did before.* The actor has succumbed to the need to be "right" out of a natural desire to be consistent with yesterday's choice.

She might then proceed to emulate yesterday's schoolgirl behavior not because of Juliet's need to run away to a new life but because of her need as an actor to satisfy a choice that everyone, particularly the actor playing Romeo, liked in the previous rehearsal. In other words, her feeling has become a *replication* of yesterday's feeling.

She's been behaving emotionally, not from a spontaneous thought-picture caused by Juliet's passion of the moment, but from her own thought caused by the need to make the so-called right choice. She has played her *interpretive opinion* of a choice that should otherwise be spontaneous.

Rehearsals are for trying out different choices to arrive at a collaborative interpretation. And Shakespeare certainly gives one plenty of room. Juliet could have been faint with fear in that moment *or* she could have been alive with adolescent blood-rush. The problem for the actor playing Juliet in the second rehearsal is that she thought the spontaneous fear of finding herself in the shadows was "wrong."

Reverse field and see what happens when the actor, unafraid of being "wrong" and willing to go with her instinct, is aware of the change in her behavior. Say the actor plays it spontaneously in rehearsal—gives in to the shadows and speaks the lines with a darkening fear.

Then say that, even though the darker choice plays well, both she and Romeo prefer what happened the day before, when Juliet behaved like a mischievous schoolgirl. Two choices, both well played.

Now what? How to assure the spontaneous repetition of the preferred choice?

To strengthen the original choice, the actor could exercise the thought-picture of the girl in the moonlight running away. Then, in rehearsal, she might suffer the fear in a dark corner of the balcony before she steps into the moonlight where a flash of the thought-picture of the little girl chasing a butterfly, reflected in the twinkle of Romeo's eyes, fills her with adolescent delight. The interpretive choice of adolescent delight has been repeated but not the feeling. The feeling is *renewed,* not repeated, and it's renewed because she's brought a resonant subtext of past and future to the moment: a portent of the future tragedy that awaits the two lovers—an intuition she'd failed to allow into the second rehearsal because she thought it was "wrong," thus denying an impulse to search for more depth in the choice.

The fact that Juliet's dread played as spontaneously as her rush to love illustrates that choices are a matter of *emphasis,* of choosing which of a character's conscious thoughts best serves the moment. Girlish impetuousness served in this interpretation. The choice of dark fear might serve the interpretation of a different production as well.

Ambition and personal style. Even though the example of the actor playing Juliet being "wrong" illustrates how a personal agenda (the need to be "right") can interrupt the flow of spontaneous feelings by inserting an inappropriate thought between a passionate response and emotional behavior, it doesn't mean actors should try to ignore their personal agendas.

On the contrary, as seen in Chapter 2, the creation of character requires the collaboration of the conscious and unconscious lives of both actor and character; it follows, therefore, that there are no boundaries on what an actor brings to the collaboration.

Moreover, a personal agenda is vital to a vigorous ambition. Without ambition an actor loses a substantial portion of the *why* to act, because the experiences, ideas, and beliefs that contribute to ambition are the foundation of personal style.

Should an actor of color not make choices relative to living in a world of white privilege because the play doesn't deal with it? Should we ask a contemporary woman not to give a contemporary spin to the interpretation of the last speech in *Taming of the Shrew* because of the patriarchal restrictions in the character's historical culture? Choices made from the actor's own era and person are natural and necessary contributions to theatre is as a living art.

Let's take a look at how one actor playing Kate can be true to her own personal style in a traditional production of the play.

Suppose the actor chose to audition because she saw a chance to satisfy a major ambition: to play Kate as a woman who demands equality of personhood before she will free herself to give love, not as a woman redeemed by romantic love as reward for being sold to the highest bidder, as suggested by the play's happy ending.

Imagine the actor, in her offstage life, is a fierce advocate of women's rights. She became a public advocate after a beloved cousin came to her with a broken cheekbone. To this day, the face of her cousin's abusive husband remains a thought-picture that produces a fury in the actor whenever she's faced with the indignities women suffer—a fury she experienced as she prepared for the audition. A fury at the root of her ambition to play Kate. (How the thought-picture of her cousin's husband has become a subtextual part of the actor's characterization of Kate will be made clear in Section 4 of the Workbook.)

Petruchio's stated action in the play is to tame Katherine, the shrew: to subject her to his authority, that she may find her "better self" as wife to husband in the name of law and love. In Shakespeare's time, the audience cheered Petruchio for bending his reluctant bride to his will. Not so the actor playing Kate. She's intent on getting her audience to cheer them both for finding a way to beat the system. She'll do it by ensuring that Kate is not merely responding to Petruchio but is pursuing an action of her own from the first time they meet. This is an intention she, the actor playing Petruchio, and the director agree on.

The actor knows it will require every skill she possesses to "tame" her fury (she loves the pun) and, at the same time, keep it as the primary motivating passion for Kate's behavior. She will have to trigger the full passion of her and Kate's rightful fury at selected moments which convey to the women (and, she hopes, men) in a contemporary audience that Kate demands the dignity of her person as a right and condition for her love.

The actor interprets Kate's dilemma thus: as soon as she meets Petruchio, he at once announces he means to marry her. Quickly, Kate realizes she'll have to frighten Petruchio off before he can gain her father's consent (which her father is sure to give). Else, she'll be bound to marry Petruchio by her father's command. The problem is, as Kate discovers right away, Petruchio can't be intimidated. Given Kate has already frightened off all other possible suitors, she's stuck with Petruchio. At least, he's a worthy adversary: strong-willed, quick of mind like her, and yes—somewhat attractive, if she were so disposed. What other choice does Kate have but to beat him at his own game? She will test whether he loves her or her dowry. She will consent to love if he will consent that they be equals in marriage. If not, he'd better watch out.

The actor has found a place in every scene to express the full, dangerous force of Kate's fury. Let's take two examples: one from their first meeting and another from the end of the play when they go off to their marriage bed together.

The actor's Kate is onto his flattery from the moment they first meet in Act II, Scene 1. Petruchio woos her as the "the prettiest Kate in Christendom" and in the next breath he tests her to see how much she will take by saying what is obviously untrue: that he has heard Kate's "mildness praised in every town," her "virtues spoke of," her "beauty sounded." Petruchio goes on to say he is moved to woo her because he sees her mildness, virtue, and beauty more deeply than anyone else could.

Kate takes up the challenge. They trade wit for wit, pun for pun, so well they enjoy it even as they battle each other for control of their futures. But Kate becomes leery as the punning takes on direct sexual allusions, and when Petruchio crosses the line with a vulgar, sexual pun, "What, with my tongue in your tail?" Kate slaps him with her full and dangerous fury. In the time-honored use of the aside in Shakespeare, Kate flashes a brief look of full, genuine rage at the audience, then quickly whips it on Petruchio as if he were her cousin's abusive husband. In that flicker of time, audience and Petruchio know this is something more than fun. Petruchio accepts Kate's challenge and responds with a broad smile as he says, "I swear

I'll cuff you if you strike again" in a soft tone of admiration. A bit further in their verbal tussles, Petruchio lets Kate know her father has already given his consent. Before Kate can vent her fury, Petruchio eases into an apparently well-meant proposal that he wants to marry her because he loves her. Just then, Petruchio has seen Kate's father approaching with two suitors for Bianca, her younger sister, who's not free to marry until Kate does. Petruchio, immediately and loudly, for all the company to hear as they enter, declares he will "tame" Kate and make her "…conformable, as other household Kates." Kate's father asks Petruchio how the wooing's coming along. Whereupon, Kate visits the full magnitude of her rage on her father. Petruchio assures the father that Kate has agreed, and they will be wed on Sunday. Kate, her fury at its peak, says she'll see him hanged first.

It would seem the game is over. Kate will be married against her will to a misogynist. So, why does Shakespeare simply say Kate and Petruchio exit with no hint of struggle between them? Because Petruchio's response assures Kate the game is still on with a clear understanding of the stakes between them. He placates her father, and the suitors, by telling them it's for he and Kate to agree between themselves, and Kate's intransigence is simply her way of going about it. This interpretation gives the two actors an opportunity to work the exit and show father, suitors, and the audience, the game will go on for the rest of the play. Petruchio heads for the exit, but Kate does not follow. Petruchio turns to look at the unmoving Kate and smiles. Kate smiles back. Petruchio leaves, knowing she will follow. Kate looks from Petruchio to the others, rises to her full and haughty height with an expression that says, "If I marry this man, it will be on my terms. What do you think of that?" and exits to continue the game for better or worse.

Let's jump ahead to the last scene, Act V, Scene 2, where Petruchio wagers he will show Lucentio and Hortensio, whose wives have already turned shrew, that he has "tamed" Kate.

The question for the actor playing Kate is how to be true to her interpretation and play the final scene of Kate's complete obedience to Petruchio. The actor's answer is to play it joyfully. The still-chaste Kate is by now fully convinced Petruchio's love is genuine. She's equally convinced that he, like her, is not bound to believe a marriage ought to be one of master and servant as law and custom demand. These certainties free Kate to anticipate a joyful marriage of communion. Hence, the actor can bring a spontaneous feeling of joy to the scene.

But there's a hitch. For practical reasons, they'll have to convince the others that Kate is, indeed, a dutiful wife in order to prove she and Petruchio are no threat to social order. Hence, Petruchio's ploy of the wager that, if successful, will add twenty thousand crowns to her dowry and insure his and Kate's independence.

By the last scene, a contemporary audience has become accustomed to Kate and Petruchio playing what we might now call, "The Taming Game." They recognize that the sly looks and artful gestures exchanged between Petruchio and Kate signal that Kate's seeming capitulation to being a dutiful wife is merely a scheme to assure Petruchio wins the wager. They get it when Kate and Petruchio share a laugh when Kate tramples her wedding cap as he has instructed her. They get it when Kate instructs the other wives to give "love, fair looks, and true obedience" in tribute to their husbands, delivered with such unbounded joy it seems to the others onstage that Kate is, indeed, "tamed."

The actor's next choice must be to make it crystal clear to the audience that Kate has achieved love on equal terms.

When Petruchio calls, "Come, Kate, we'll to bed," she rushes to him and hops on his back as if to ride him like horse. And a moment later, when Petruchio bids them all a good night, Kate mock-whips him with the mangled marriage cap, and off they go—as the audience laughs, knowing Kate is likely to carry her zest for independence to her marriage bed with a guarantee it will be an engagement of equals.

The actor has maintained the essence of her own personal style by creating a character motivated by her personal ambition to right injustice visited on women. And she's done it and stayed faithful to the time and culture of the play.

The next chapter illustrates how to express the emotional behavior of a character as feeling in action.

Chapter 5
Emotional Behavior as Feeling in Action

While off-stage life is mainly about avoiding crisis, a play is mainly about dealing with crisis. As a play seeks to resolve a crisis, emotional behavior, expressed as feeling in action, can be positive or negative. A positive feeling is one which leads, knowingly or unknowingly, toward a resolution of crisis. A negative feeling is one which works against it.

As we understand passion to be the ontological source of feelings, feelings are also charged with positive or negative passions. The interplay between positive and negative passions and their expressions of emotional behavior as feelings provide rhythm, tempo, suspense, and surprise during the play's attempt to create and resolve a crisis.

But life is not a play. For most of life, most people spend most of every day trying to avoid any trouble that might lead to a crisis. They cross the street to avoid surly strangers. They screen their calls to avoid bill-collectors and telemarketers. They turn down invitations to love because relationships are too demanding. They get in the habit of avoiding trouble for fear of facing the possibility that Albert Collins touched on when he sang, "Nobody loves me but my mama, and I ain't too sure about her."

It is, of course, perfectly reasonable to avoid trouble in the interest of self-preservation. But a too-constant fear of trouble and its consequences risks habitual unwillingness to engage crisis, which can too easily become a *habit of not wanting.* Listen to how often people use mantras like "I wish this would go away" or "I don't want anything to do with this."

Actors naturally have their own habits of negative feelings—gremlins of *not wanting* that lurk in the subconscious waiting for a chance to distract the actor's concentration with mantras such as "Can't I cut that line?" "I don't want to lose the audience," "I don't want to overact," or a director's pet peeve: "People don't behave that way."

Emotional behavior without passion as its source lacks genuine energy and suspense.

Positive use of negative feelings. When carried from life to stage, the habit of not wanting is an actor's enemy. On the other hand, negative feelings brought from life can have interpretive value. To have inner conflict, a fully dimensional character *must* have negative feelings. This calls for an actor to make a distinction between negative feelings that serve as motivation for character behavior and negative feeling *habits* carried from life to stage.

Keats' famous postulation of "negative capability" can serve as something of a guide to rid the work of unhelpful, personal negative thoughts and leave an actor free to use a character's negative thoughts in positive ways to create a fully dimensional character. Keats asserted that artistic achievement comes about when one is "capable of being in uncertainties, Mysteries, doubts, without any irritable reaching after fact & reason."

In Chapter 2, I talked about an actor arriving at a unique characterization by first surrendering to the passion of the character's life with all its uncertainties, mysteries, and doubts. As Keats would make a poem from his surrender to the beauty of a Grecian urn, an actor would recreate the beauty of a character, first formed as dramatic literature, as an in-the-flesh character alive with *feeling in action*. That surrender can be thought of as a "negative capability," because it is absent any reason not to surrender. Therefore, the actor is more *capable* of making positive uses of a character's negative thoughts, and his own, as positive additions to the beauty of a character's portrait.

Here's a look at how an actor playing Romeo can use a negative feeling from his own life to affect choices appropriate to his characterization. As you watch the actor find his choices in the following illustrations, presume he interprets

Romeo's tragedy not only as love oppressed but also as rebellion thwarted.

Suppose the actor brings an active anger from a recent break-up after a year-long relationship into Act I, Scene 1, in which his friend Benvolio tries to snap Romeo out of the lovesick despair of his unrequited love for Rosaline by asking, "Dost thou not laugh?" Romeo's response is both positive and negative: *positive* as it expresses the character's desire of the moment (to indulge his despair) when he answers, "No, coz, I'd rather weep," and *negative* in his refusal to snap out of it, that is, *not wanting* the action Benvolio offers.

Presume, for a moment, the actor has already created a thought-picture in his mind's eye of Rosaline as "the envious moon"—that same moon Romeo speaks of later in the balcony scene.

Now, suppose the actor's animus toward his first lover that makes him flash on a picture of an imagined Rosaline as the visual image of the thought *how could she do this to me?* Almost immediately the actor realizes he's made an inappropriate choice. His personal anger is at cross purposes with his interpretation. Romeo's essentially comic need to romanticize his adolescent grief at being jilted is needed here as a contrast to highlight his later choice that Romeo's rebellion against the restraints of his time and place is born from his love for Juliet. How to deal with the actor's misplaced anger?

Imagine that the actor recalls the moment of silence immediately after his real-life lover announced she wanted to break it off. And imagine that, in that moment, he saw in her a look of genuine concern for him—a look that made him heartsick at losing her. Say that he recognizes, now, this feeling of heartsickness that his anger had not allowed him to acknowledge at the time.

Now the actor has a thought, grounded in personal memory, that activates a feeling reason to say *I'd rather weep.* The actor has changed a negative feeling to a positive one: to share a lovesickness appropriate to both actor and character.

Not coincidentally, the actor's choice of Romeo's naivete here and his later choice of rebellion are worthy of Shakespeare's masterful use of the contrasting forces of light and dark, moon and sun, that provide the play its tragic suspense.

The actor has not denied the validity of his personal experience as useful to his interpretation of Romeo. Instead, he has changed his thought process to express emotional behavior appropriate to character. The anger of his personal experience remains as a useful, subtextual nuance of Romeo's romantic grief. (The craft that makes this possible, we'll deal with in the Workbook.)

Let's move ahead to Scenes 1 and 2 of Act II to see how the actor brings that subtextual anger into positive play as the spirit of Romeo's rebellion so dear to his interpretation.

In Scene 1 of Act II, Romeo overcomes a moment's hesitation and goes over the orchard wall to pursue his forbidden love for Juliet. Immediately, Benvolio and Mercutio, in pursuit of Romeo, call to him from the other side of the wall to join them for a night of fun.

When he hears Mercutio conjure Rosaline by name, the actor does not play Romeo's heartsickness. This time he chooses to introduce Romeo's rebellious anger. He feels a flash of anger brought on by the thought-picture of Rosaline as the envious moon.

Scene 2 begins immediately after Benvolio and Mercutio exit. The actor interprets the abrupt change from Scene 1 to Scene 2, in which no time passes, as Shakespeare's way to signify that Romeo is acting impulsively from a state of radically conflicted feelings. The immediate departure of Benvolio and Mercutio has left Romeo not with thoughts of Juliet but with mixed feelings of the pain of Rosaline's rejection and anger at Mercutio for taunting him. These feelings of pain and anger he directs to the absent Mercutio with "He jests at scars that never felt a wound." The moment is played for two reasons of value to the actor's interpretation: to contrast his romantic love for Rosaline with what will be his tragic love for Juliet—a love that rebels against any force that would deny it.

We can see how this positive choice of the once-negative feeling affects the desired interpretation throughout the balcony scene.

In the following soliloquy, a conflicted Romeo sometimes speaks of Juliet, sometimes of Rosaline, and sometimes of both as one. For example, with "what light through yonder window breaks," Romeo sees Juliet as the "fair sun," and in a radical flash he sees Rosaline as the envious moon, which causes him to call for the fair sun to "kill the envious moon." Romeo uses the next five lines to "cast off" the "sick and green" envious moon that is "pale with grief" and drive the fickle Rosaline from his mind. An action that frees him to announce his love for Juliet: "It is my lady; O, it is my love!"

By the end of the soliloquy, when he sees Juliet touch her cheek with a pained and sorrowful longing, Romeo wishes he could be a glove upon her hand that he might touch her cheek! Hope is raised that she requites his love when she speaks for the first time and he hears the music of her same longing as she says, "Ay me!" And when he entreats her to speak again, he speaks not of the envious moon (Rosaline) but "glorious night"—a portent of the unimagined dark end that awaits the lovers.

Romeo is ready to respond to the chord of unspoken rebellion in his heart when he hears Juliet wishing aloud for Romeo to "Deny thy father and refuse thy name!" or, if he won't, she will deny her name for love of him. He is both thrilled and frightened at the boldness of Juliet's love, colored as it is with rebellion and the danger of consequence. He dares not reveal himself until he hears Juliet call on her imagined Romeo to "doff thy name; / And for that name, which is no part of thee, / Take all myself."

Juliet's daring offer of her youthful heart, soul, and body, in complete abandonment to love, fills Romeo with so trembling an excitement of feeling, he now declares aloud to his beloved that he is "new baptized" as love itself and no more Romeo or Montague. (A profound irony Shakespeare has set up earlier when Romeo tells Benvolio, "Tut, I have lost myself; I am not here;/ This is not Romeo, he's some other where.")

For the rest of the scene, played in the "mask of night," the two actors pay honor to the brilliance of the writing: they play Romeo and Juliet as daring, bantering, teasing, erotic, mischievous, innocent, rebellious, fearful of the future, yet brave to create a new world consecrated by love.

This marvelous complex swirl of feelings, which so elegantly captures the comic tone of youthful innocence and the tragic tone of inevitable doom, has come alive because the actor used a version of his own negative feeling when appropriate for the character.

No small parts. To be stage-worthy, all characters need behave with this interplay between positive and negative feelings.

The supporting part of the drunken Porter in Macbeth, for example, is so busy with his negative version of Dante's *Inferno* that he refuses to answer the knocking at the gate. It's only when he realizes it's too cold in Macbeth's castle for him to be in Hell that he joins the play with a positive action to open the gate to let the play take its course. Even a character who appears to be unnecessary to the resolution of the play has positive feelings of their own: a minor character of an aging butler in a drawing room comedy might behave with a seeming indifference to the events of the play, but in the play of his own life, his thoughts might look forward to his coming day off as he imagines lifting his laughing grandchild off the ground. Such positive thoughts might add subtextual nuance of delightful anticipation to the atmosphere of the scene, thereby bringing truth to the old cliché: there are no small parts, only small actors.

Before we get into the nitty-gritty of the exercises in the Workbook, and for the pleasure of looking ahead to where and how a mastery of craft pays off, let's take a look at how an actor, working at his craft, is inspired by a serendipitous discovery in rehearsal.

Chapter 6
Inspiration

A day before the first dress rehearsal of *The Glass Menagerie*, everyone in the company is confident of success. Everyone, that is, except the actor playing Tom Wingfield. Some little thing is missing. He knows not what. Too many times during the last run-through he'd been conscious he was acting. He hadn't fully "dropped down" into the character, as he likes to think of it. Something was missing. The director told him he was asking too much of himself, trying to be perfect, he should just relax, it'll happen, the audience will do it for him, that's what previews are for. It's true the actor is inclined to overwork things, always looking to be his best. But, this time, he doesn't buy the director's well-meaning advice. This time, he really is after whatever it is that's missing. He feels it floating vaguely through and around his bones…a phantom teasing him…an answer tantalizing him… What the hell is it? Where the hell is it?

On his way home after rehearsal, he goes into the Columbus Library on 10th Avenue, which he does once in a while when he wants a quiet place to sit and think. Running the day's rehearsal in his mind, he notices that the places he'd felt not quite *there* happened in the scenes with Tom's mother. He'd felt completely present every moment with his sister, Laura. Ah! The missing thread is in the relationship with his mother, Amanda—a relationship legendary in American theatre for its illumination of the synergy between mother and male child. Convinced he knows where to look, the actor goes home to work.

Inside his apartment, he opens a beer and works through his somewhat rumpled, marked up, pale blue covered copy of the play, looking for any places he might have misinterpreted Tom's behavior. Nope. He and the director are simpatico on every beat in the play. If not a bad choice, what then? Has he harbored an unconscious fear of something in the part or in the relationship with Tom's mother? He can't think of anything. But just going through the script again gives him the feeling he's on the right track—a feeling that moves him from worry to working mode. He'll try a couple of exercises to see if he can shake something out. He figures that Tom's opening speech to the audience, when he ruminates on the fire escape about the most significant event of his life, might be where he finds what he's looking for.

The actor calls on two exercises that have been helpful with past characters. First, he changes locations for the scene in the hope a different intention, with a different listener, in a different place with a different atmosphere, will prompt a discovery. The actor has Tom say it to a stranger as if he were drunk in a dive bar at 3 a.m., to no apparent result. He tries a few others, like Tom offering the speech as a toast to his best friend's wedding at a Miami Beach resort. None of them help. Next, in an appeal to his unconscious to show him a clue, he tries the ad-lib exercise. He has Tom say the speech as he does in the play. This time through, the actor ad-libs aloud: a no-holds-barred, improvised response to how Tom feels from one major beat in the speech to the next. Alas, no matter how he works the speech, whatever he's looking for remains out of reach. He's forced to admit he is overworking this time. He's done this enough to know exercise may not always have an immediate result, but the work will often contribute to a spontaneous, playable choice during rehearsal.

So next, the actor playing Tom turns to what he often does when he finds himself working too hard: he goes to the other arts for inspiration. He rereads passages from Saramago's *Blindness*; he immerses himself in his catalogue of Rothko paintings as he listens to Satie's *Gymnopedie*.

Despite the fact the exercises have yielded nothing tangible, the work itself and the visits to the other arts have relaxed him, moved him somewhere else inside himself, and left the actor playing Tom looking forward to tomorrow's dress rehearsal.

During Act I, Scene 3, of the once-dreaded first dress rehearsal, something happens just before the famous Blue Mountain speech to make the words burst forth from Tom with more power and resonance than the actor had ever expressed before. Tom's need to free himself from his mother and obey his passion for adventure are suddenly released, phrase after phrase, with pain, wit, and ferocity. Amanda is stunned by Tom's attack, and he sees in her eyes that she *knows* how much he hurts. He sees how much she suffers, how much she loves her son! And he sees, too, that he has shaken her to the core, made her see the truth of herself for the first time in her life, and how afraid she is to lose him. And still he cannot stop attacking her because he also sees how "this dreadful affliction of love," as Tennessee Williams called it, has bound them together, has turned his mother into a monster who is destroying his sister and suffocating his own will to live. All his love, his need, his ambition, guilt, and fury, come pouring out in a relentless assault until the final explosion that sends his mother "up, up, up on a broomstick, over Blue Mountain with seventeen gentlemen callers! You ugly babbling old witch!"

When the scene is over, the character Tom Wingfield goes off to a bar in a remorseful fury and gets drunk, while the actor remains offstage, mumbling over and over to himself with a feeling near to glee, "That's it! I've got it! That's it! That's him! He's here."

The actor has, at last, *become* the character. He feels it in his whole being. On stage, his blood pulsed, his adrenaline rushed. His whole body *was* Tom. And still is. Or rather there are two of him now.

One of him, the Tom of him, seems in some sense to be everywhere at once. He can feel himself sitting in a bar in Depression-era St. Louis woozily counting his change to make sure he's saved enough to go to the movies, and at the same time he can smell the jonquil aroma of Amanda's cheap perfume in their dingy, dark apartment and hear the music from the Paradise dance hall across the back alley. He can still see the scratched old Victrola below the picture of his long-gone father on the wall, can feel his heart breaking at what he has done to his mother and sister. He feels his Tom-heart breaking across time and place, even as his actor-mind gallops with hypotheticals, frantically trying to grasp an objective view of what "dropped him down" into the whole of Tom. What was it that caused that awful recognition in Amanda's eyes? Had Tom been motivated by the anguish of being trapped in the Celotex interior of the warehouse? Possibly, but that's only one of the many motivations driving Tom to attack his mother. And, of course, it could have been…whoa, whoa. Hold it. Wrong track. The actor playing Tom realizes there is no single, logical understanding of motive to explain what happened to let his body "drop down" into the character. Maybe it was just the sheer force and beauty of Tennessee Williams' language. Perhaps it was as simple as will power, just get it done, damn it! No—wait, wait…will power?... no, it wasn't will power. It felt more like he had surrendered to something. But surrendered to what? The actor is reluctant to chalk his good fortune up to serendipity. He fears the moment won't happen again unless he can nail down that *something*— that moment of inspiration he can use to keep the whole of Tom's presence with him.

Standing in the wings, he can almost feel the racing synapses of his brain spur his mind to run the whole scene up to the moment of the Blue Mountain speech as he just played it. What am I looking for? he thinks, as the scene fast forwards in his mind. Oh my God, stop! Run it back. There, freeze it there! Yes! There it is! How simple! How magnificently simple. It's my wrist! It's my right wrist.

He smiles as he realizes how, in previous rehearsals, he would jam both fists into his sides as bitter parody of his mother's "Rise and shine! Rise and shine!" But now he knows he'd got the gesture wrong. The actor playing Amanda had *not* jammed both fists into her sides, as he'd thought. Rather, the actor playing Amanda had placed both hands in her usual manner: elbows crooked, forearms jammed into her waist, with *both wrist bones crooked inward, palms open, fingers splayed!* —a gesture of moral judgement as she announced she had taken "that hideous book by that insane Mr. Lawrence" back to the library. This is the moment—the words, the gesture—which sent Tom into the fury that changed all their lives forever. In today's dress rehearsal he had got Tom's version of the gesture right! His left hand was a locked fist as he jammed it into his side, but his right forearm was crooked and jammed into his right side—not in a fist but with its *wrist bone crooked inward, palms open, fingers splayed*, like his mother's!

Thrilled at his discovery, the actor gets to work immediately. He picks up his tattered blue acting edition and reads the speech aloud as he speculates the whys and wherefores, the meanings, the explanations for the gesture. But this time the search for understanding is not in search of a logic to understand motive. There is no mind—certainly not his own relatively untutored mind—capable of cataloging all the possible resonances contained in that simple, artful gesture that had been the catalyst to bring all the knowns and unknowns of Tom Wingfield's life fully into the actor's body. Rather, the quest is to keep alive the actor's intuitive connection to the fount of possible understandings about Amanda's lifelong influence on Tom's character.

So, the actor allows himself the pleasure of exercising his intellectual curiosity to ruminate on the sources of his inspiration so that he may experience the contradictory, and pleasurable, feeling of embodying what he doesn't know. If the gesture of crooking his wrist into his side borrowed from his mother is also an expression of what is unsayable about her influence on Tom, he wonders what is it that can't be said? Repressed homosexuality? Nothing in the play to indicate that. Was the gesture a cultural artifact, a Jungian symbol of the collective unconscious of woman, the *anima,* in all of us? Did the clenched fist of his left hand belong to the father in him, while the inward-bent right wrist belonged to the mother? He keeps ruminating until he intuits a need to make the gesture. Then he goes back to the feeling of rage that starts Tom's attack on Amanda. He exercises connecting the gesture to the feeling until it becomes a feeling habit. Then, to ensure the gesture is present as sub-text throughout the play, he exercises the gesture in various places in various scenes. The actor does this until he is at the ready to "drop down" into Tom consistently from the time he leaves the dressing room until he bows at curtain call.

Thus, the actor playing Tom has used his craft to inspire and used his inspiration to find craft. It's from the interplay between inspiration and craft the actor simultaneously creates a meaningful interpretation of a character made whole in flesh and bone beyond interpretation!

The following Workbook will refresh the working relationship between craft and inspiration and illustrate how to use exercise to embody a character's inner life in the movement, gesture, sound, and speech that express *spontaneous feeling behavior*.

PART TWO

A Workbook for Creating Character

Introduction to the Workbook

Here's a long sentence with nine commas that signifies the task of creating a character. Every feeling moment of character on stage is made up of passion, thought process, and emotional behavior, happening simultaneously in past, present, and future in some combination of actor and character, in a certain place that contains certain objects, under certain conditions, at a certain historical moment, within the circumstances of a given culture.

One might argue that it's nearly impossible to fully comprehend all the aspects of one moment of a character's behavior, let alone moment after moment after moment for two hours of performance, eight times a week. The hope, of course, is that the genius of inspiration will lighten the load enough to make getting the work done by opening night a reasonable possibility.

For the fun of it

A life of acting characters in the flesh requires a curiosity for the wonders of the human body. The thrill of being present in mind and spirit and body is the reward that makes the work of finding movement and gesture to express the inner life of a character such great fun.

For example, imagine an actor playing the love-smitten, lust-driven Boniface in Feydeau and Desvallières' *Hotel Paradiso* as he moves stealthily through the seedy hotel corridor to a room where Marcelle, the unhappy young wife of his friend, M. Cot, awaits, in confused anticipation, her first attempt at adultery.

Suppose the actor makes the character's entrance skulking quickly on tiptoe, one hand using the wall to guide and support him. But then he stops suddenly at the sound of a doorknob clicking somewhere along the corridor. He holds completely still, fearful of being discovered. False alarm. All clear. Boniface is about to continue down the corridor in prospect of a consummated romance with an eager and breathless Marcelle. What a marvelous moment the click of that doorknob!

Does Boniface stop and turn immediately upon hearing the soft click of the doorknob? Does he stop, hold, not turn at all? Turn halfway? Turn very slowly? Then, another delicious moment of choice occurs when Boniface is assured there is no danger. What does the character do before he continues his move down the corridor of the Hotel Paradiso? Does he smooth back his hair because the moment of fright has disturbed his vanity? Does he remember he's wearing his spectacles and take them off? Does he lick his lips because his mouth is dry from fear? And then, how has his movement changed after the mysterious click? Will he walk on tiptoe to be even more quiet? Will he hold his hands in front of him like a blind person groping his way in the dark? Or does he rise to his full height of five feet three inches, extend his paunch proudly as if it were his priapic member, and walk boldly, in measured cadence, on his heels, toward his clandestine assignation?

The scene has offered a fun-filled opportunity to discover character choice, possible only if the actor's body is prepared to respond in character.

Inspiration and craft

In *The Hidden Order of Art,* Anton Ehrenzweig writes that the foundation for a creative imagination is our childlike ability to experience intuitive, freeform associations between the conscious and the unconscious. In addition, he advises that our socially educated thought processes—without which we could not invent sequential and systematic disciplines—ought not to censor us but, rather, should buddy up with us to unleash the power of our creative imagination. In other words, the intuitive and the rational are partners.

I refer to the work process as craft because, although it is considered synonymous with technique, I find it better expresses the artisanal sense of the labor that goes into the art of creating character.

That said, the labor of exercise too often seems irritating, boring, dangerous physically and psychologically, and time-consuming. But it need not be. The basic purpose of exercise is to prepare an actor's mind, body, and spirit to function at its optimal human ability. Once trained, the actor will use the range of those abilities in whatever degree is required for the interpretation of how the character reacts to the dangers of crisis. In other words, exercise is no more than an unnatural way to ready the body for expressing natural behavior—internal and external, critical or otherwise.

An athlete, while training for a marathon, will feel the animal thrill of adding a half mile toward the ultimate goal of 26 miles, 385 yards. When an actor trains with the "unnatural" exercise of craft, they will feel the animal thrill of being fully present in thought, word, and deed as if it were as natural as a sunrise.

So, the actor who is instructed to repeat, to go over and over, again and again, can take heart. The reward for the work of exercise is the fun of search and discovery and the physical thrill of behaving "in character" with ease.

To that end, the Workbook contains a series of exercises meant to facilitate a clear understanding of what's involved in the making of character. The exercises are presented as a series, from the beginning to the end of the work sequence, preceded by a brief note explaining context.

As we use this approach for a guide, it's wise to remember that too strict a logical approach to acting can stifle the free flow of creative imagination inspired by play and character.

Once craft has been mastered, any one of the exercises can be used at any time as the need occurs in rehearsals or to refresh performance.

Some of the exercises are of my own invention and some are reworkings from my point of view of exercises that have become historical contributions to the vocabulary of acting.

While the exercises use different actors in different plays, playing different characters, as illustrations of the work, an actor should use them to create their own singular interpretation of the one character they are working on.

The first three exercises deal with preparing the body for rehearsals. The middle five concern creating character before and during rehearsals. The next to last ensures that all behavior is spontaneous. The last deals with shaping the performance into an aesthetic whole, ready for an audience.

They all work on the premise that body and voice are the craft tools to express the emotional behavior described in Part One. The preceding précis serve to place them in context with the entirety of the work to be done. Each step of every exercise is thoroughly detailed, accompanied with more specific comment as needed.

As we start the Workbook by putting observation to work, keep in mind the thrill the actor playing Tom Wingfield felt when his body became *fully present in character*, and how his use of exercise culminated in the ultimately inexplicable pleasure of being there.

Index of Exercises

The Line Exercise   60
An Exercise to Habituate Extremes of Feeling   63
An Exercise to Embody Passion   69
An Exercise for the Body Within   78
An Exercise for Instinctive Life Habits   89
An Exercise for Learned Character Habits   94
An Exercise for Speaking in Character   110
An Exercise for Breathing in Character   122
An Exercise of Place   130
An Exercise to Improvise Possible Choices   138
An Exercise to Improvise Irrational Thought Process   145
An Exercise to Establish a Feeling Basis or Habits
           of Behavior   152
An Exercise to Create a Template of Still Life Portraits   154
An Exercise to Create a Moving Portrait of Character   158

1.
The Power of Observation

Context

The body is always alive with feeling. It's never completely still, even at rest. In sleep, it will twitch, toss and turn, sometimes make gestures in response to dreams, and, when awake, it's always at least blinking and breathing— contracting and expanding with the simple involuntary tasks of staying alive.

A great many theatre practitioners have made significant contributions to the artful use of the body in performance. Much of the exercise work on physical behavior I offer is influenced by and adapted from the work of three of those artists: Francois Delsarte (as passed on by Ted Shawn), Michael Chekov, and Jean-Louis Barrault.

Before I offer a way to read body language using elements of what has come to be called the Delsarte System, a bit of background will help for context.

In the latter half of the nineteenth century, Delsarte, a French singer, became convinced that the damage to his voice, which had ended his career, was caused by training that lacked knowledge of the body's function in vocal expression. He then devoted his life to codifying and teaching a system of "laws" that would train performers to express with ease a truthful physical reflection of every human feeling. He died before he could finish recording what he called the Laws of Expression, but some of his students kept notes in hopes of passing on the master's work.

The Delsarte system found its most effective practitioner when, in 1915, Ted Shawn revived it not for acting but for dance. Shawn used his grasp of the Delsarte system to make a major contribution to a new art form called Modern Dance.

With the caveat that hypothetical generalizations invite exceptions and a reminder that the proof is in the playing, let's look at the ways the body can serve the actor as a laboratory for expressing character. Here's a somewhat simplistic vocabulary, influenced by Delsarte, that provides a basis for reading body language. I offer it with the understanding that an accurate, comprehensive interpretation of a character's body behavior is not possible without the context of the character's inner life.

Principles of observation.

There are two inextricably linked ways to observe physical behavior: general (behavior common to all) and particular (behavior specific to character).

Let's start with general behavior. Physical behavior is composed of two basic elements: movement and gesture. There are three principles that form the basis for observing physical behavior.

(1) *The body in space.* Does the person observed generally contract or expand in space? Is the body in control or is it controlled by its environment?

(2) *The rhythm and tempo of movement.* Is the person fast or slow, rounded or angular? Does the person stop/start or move smoothly?

(3) *The patterns and motifs of gesture.* How often does the person tug at a belt? Does the person always cross the right leg over the left?

Now, a look at specific character behavior. There are five basic ways to read the body as a more specific guide to character behavior.

(1) *Think of the body as a left half and a right half.* The beating human heart is more to the left side of the body than the right, suggesting it's the feeling side of the body because the warmth of its first human contact is felt in the heart's blood. The rush of blood pumped *from* the heart to the right half, suggests that the right half prompts thought process, the beginning of a sense of self. These primitive body responses

suggest the left half could be emotional, impulsive, rebellious, radical, and so on; the right thoughtful, willful, strong, tyrannical, reasonable, etcetera.

(2) *The fleshier parts of the body hold more emotion than the bonier parts.* Putting the palms of the hands to the cheeks is a more emotional gesture than putting the back of the hand to the forehead. A gangster giving a backhand to a snitch is colder than a wife's open-handed slap to the face of an errant husband. Casanova may shock a prospective conquest when he turns over her offered hand and kisses its palm.

(3) Similarly, *the outer parts of the body that habitually protect it from external physical danger are less expressive of feeling than the protected parts.* Note the difference in feeling when putting the hands under the arms after crossing them, and then crossing them and putting the hands on the outside of the arms. Notice, as well, the difference of feeling when putting the hands between the thighs or on the flanks.

(4) *The use of the joints reflects the amount and intensity of will, authority, and power being exercised.* Locking the joints and/or firming them up indicates more intensity. Get someone to leave a room by flapping your hands and shooing them away, or firm up the wrists, turn the person around, and push the person out.

(5) *The fingertips are expressive of the intellect; they are antennae of the human body that comprehend by touch.* Imagine a student taking a difficult test. It would seem likely she'd find the correct answer if she were tapping her forehead with her fingertips. It would seem she might be too worried to pass it if the fingers of her hand were massaging her cheeks and mouth.

With this general understanding of how to observe the body, let's take a look at an actor who makes an observant study of a woman sitting hunched over a library table reading a book.

The woman takes a drink of water from a glass to her left, puts the glass back on the table, and resumes reading. Did what she was reading cause her to hunch forward or raise her head at a certain point? Was there a rhythmic sense from reading to reaching to drinking to returning to read? Did she drink in a slow or fast tempo? Did she put the glass back in the same place?

This first observation will give an alert actor a feel, a general sense of the woman's character. Think of this sense as a first read in need of further investigation. A hypothesis in need of proof.

Now, the actor goes on a search for specific character behavior.

The woman, after a moment, turns a page, hunches forward ever so slightly more as she gets increasingly immersed in what she reads. Then she slides her right hand along the table, palm down, to the glass of water, which she picks up—not by the usual gesture of wrapping her fingers around the body of the glass with the palm of her hand but by picking it up by the rim with her fingertips. The glass seems to rise from the table like a helicopter before it floats to her lips for two sips. The woman has not taken her eyes from the book except for the moment it takes to place the glass to her lips. She continues to read. Still holding the glass with her fingertips, she pushes it with her right arm back to its original position. All the time reading.

What does this reveal about the woman? A cornucopia of possibilities. Maybe she's reading dispassionately, because she picked the glass up with her fingertips and not the whole of her hand. She might be a sensuous person, as well, because she embraced the table by sliding her hand across, palm down. She's doing two things at once, reading a book and reaching for the water—she might have a capacity for multitasking. Is she blind to the world because she works with feel and not sight? Or is she simply trusting of that world around her?

It's not necessary, or even wise, to answer the questions that arise from a general exercise of reading body language. No matter how great the intellectual temptation to interpret them, the questions are better used as agents for storing the observations in a warehouse of body memories available for use later.

Laurence Olivier, considered by many to be the greatest English-speaking actor of his generation, once remarked on the pleasure he took in observing people's walks, and how a remembered walk would often arrive serendipitously from the memory bank of his unconscious. One might say, with almost certainty, that Olivier's every-which-way body movements and batting of eyes in his performance of Archie Rice, the song and dance man in *The Entertainer*, were the conscious character choices of a fine actor. But would the choices, resonant of multiple interpretations—among them a man lost to his own body and seeking approval for an inner self equally lost—have been possible without the aid of his memory bank of body walks, created by a lifetime of keen observation?

With powers of observation refreshed, the actor is ready to prepare the body to make intuitive and spontaneous choices from a collection of body memories that will express character behavior unique to the actor's interpretation.

2.
Preparing the Actor's Body

Context

A deer feeding on a shrub, upon hearing the faintest noise or catching the slightest scent, will raise its head, prick its ears, hold still to find the direction of danger, flash its white tail as a warning flag to others, and move quickly to safety. Nothing fussy there. Each gesture has purpose, and the combined gestures accumulate energy toward a movement. Economy and simplicity in the face of danger.

The body in reaction to crisis

In crisis, all creatures marshal the full power of their animal forces as best they can toward a simple action of survival. But for the human animal it's not as simple as it seems.

A play moves toward a crisis. A character faces the unfolding crisis with feeling behavior in the present that is influenced by a history of past behavior. The degree of intensity of each feeling happens on a scale of one to a hundred from the beginning of the play to its climax. Therefore, every movement and gesture also reflect a degree of suspense compatible with how near or far the character is to the moment of reckoning that leads to the climax.

Interpretation and crisis

An interpretation requires a scale of intensity relative to crisis, determined by what might be called a hierarchy of values. A character is governed by a construct of values—conscious and unconscious, chosen, inherited, wanted, unwanted—a construct that appears to make one moment more valuable than another. But no moment should be taken for granted as if it has a lesser value to the action toward the play's crisis. Each moment has a value (despite the level of intensity) that makes it special because *it happens in the present.*

The simple act of opening a door, for example, is more than an everyday activity. The poet, playwright, and filmmaker Jean Cocteau observed that when you open a door, the outside world rushes in, and when you close one, the world is shut out.

How circumstance affects the value of a moment relative to the crisis is what determines its intensity. To illustrate the distinction, imagine a circumstance in which a character bursts into the house jumping for joy at having won the lottery. Then suppose the character's lover, who has been secretly looking for a way to end their affair, replies with considerably less intensity of feeling, "Well, that's good news." The choice of not wanting a confrontation in this circumstance does not lessen the feeling value of the lover's need to end the relationship. Rather, the lover's need remains an *active presence* that lowers the intensity of the character's response to the other lover's good news. What makes the choice spontaneous is the actor's *habit of bringing the full value to* the need for ending the relationship. Thus, the *lowered intensity* of feeling toward the good news adds suspense as the scene moves both characters toward their inevitable crisis.

External expression of inner feeling

With respect for Rodin's desire to have the body mirror the soul, the next two exercises are meant to prepare the actor's body to reflect the appropriate external expressions of the character's inner life.

The reward is to enjoy the sheer athletic pleasure of choosing movements and gestures appropriate to the feeling life of an interpretation: choices true to a character's past and present behavior, and pregnant with suspense for what the character will do next.

For starters, here's a look at a Michael Chekov exercise, with my own variations, designed to prepare the actor's body *to be in the habit* of responding to the full value of even the most seemingly casual moment.

The Line Exercise

1. Stand immediately behind an imaginary line on the floor.

The imaginary line reminds us that offstage and onstage are different and that each moment has its own special place, its own stage. It's important to go *immediately* from one step to the other in the exercise. The objective is to capture the full value of one moment, unaffected by what went before and what will come after. One move, one gesture, and we are not in the same place as we were just a moment ago.

2. Think of the first thing to say and/or do that comes to mind.

3. In your mind (not out loud) say, "This is the beginning."

To announce "the beginning" is to raise the curtain on the moment and only the moment.

4. Step over the line and say or do the first thing that comes to mind.

The saying or doing of the moment thus becomes rarefied. (Do this exercise often enough and an actor will experience the air get lighter and cooler on the playing side of the line.)

5. Step back behind the line and in your mind (not out loud) say, "This is the end."

To announce "the end" is to bring the curtain down and preserve the unaffected value of the moment in body memory.

Uses for interpretation

Repetition of the exercise will *imbue behavior with character habit.* Suppose the first thing the actor thinks of for Boniface to do is have a habit of cleaning out his ear with his little finger.

After habituating the gesture, the actor could single out discreetly chosen moments to use the gesture as a signifier that Boniface is a man who does not wish to hear what he does not want to hear. For example, when Marcelle tells Boniface she's afraid her husband will discover them, he might unconsciously dig the wax out of his ear as he assures her that no one in their circle could ever imagine they would meet for a tryst at Hotel Paradiso.

Other uses

The Line Exercise can also be used to make *the body rule the reluctant mind*—as when character behavior (physical or verbal) may seem foreign to the actor, or when the actor may shy from a certain kind of behavior.

Suppose that the actor playing Boniface, after the serendipitous discovery of the gesture, thought sticking his finger in his ear too vulgar and didn't want to keep it. But persuaded by the director it was a funny and telling habit, he used the Line Exercise to habituate his body to do what his mind initially rebelled against as vulgar behavior.

The exercise should also be used indiscriminately as general practice for the acting instrument. Step over the line and say and/or do anything for the sheer fun of it. The upshot is that the habit of giving moments their full value, individually at random, will insure the actor against the pitfall of slighting moments played with lesser intensity.

Having observed the body as a starting point for interpretation and used the Line Exercise to create the habit of giving full value to every moment, the actor is ready to habituate the body to the capacity for extreme feelings in moments of crisis.

3.
Extreme Feeling

Context

Imagine a comic scene in which a father is taking his turn to change a diaper in the middle of the night. He enters in a slow shuffle, groggily resigned to performing his parental duty. It's not a crisis. He'd rather go back to bed. The groggy father gets a laugh bumblingly opening a closet door in the dark. Then the scene turns serious when the father hears the child gasping for breath. He runs to his child's aid as quickly as he can. But the actor makes a mistake.

He hears the child gasping and, emboldened by the first laugh, he improvises a second sight gag by bumping into and catching a falling lamp. He sets it back and continues his rush to the rescue. But no laugh. Why not? Because the actor's mind refused his body's instinctive response to crisis to make room for a gag. His response to the extremity of his child's danger is not genuine, and the audience knows it.

Could the actor have satisfied his intention to get an added laugh and still make the reaction to the child's gasping genuine? Yes. If his body's instinct to save the child had been stronger than his self-conscious need for another laugh, he would not have realized he'd knocked the lamp over. Stopping to set the lamp right betrayed that the actor cared more about the laugh than the father did for his child. The actor would have gotten his desired laugh if his body had mindlessly caught the lamp on the fly and carried it with him to the rescue. And the behavior, comic in spirit, would have emphasized the urgency of the crisis. Furthermore, he may garner another laugh if he appears with a prideful smile at having saved his child, unmindful he is still holding the lamp. And yet another laugh is possible if, on his exit, he realizes he's taking the lamp to bed with him, then stops and puts it back with as much care as he practiced when taking care of his child.

The actor has realized four potential laughs in the scene with an instinctive, truthful response of extreme feeling to the critical moment of the scene. And, at the same time, the actor's physical behavior further characterizes the father in a manner true to the comic spirit of the play.

The following exercise combines variations of Michael Chekov's and Jean Louis Barrault's ways of concentrating energy to prepare the body to habituate the *potential for extreme feeling* so it can react with any degree of intensity as the crisis leads to the climax of the play.

The premise for the exercise is that the body reacts to a stimulus in two fundamental ways: contraction and expansion. A bad feeling causes a contraction, like a punch in the gut. A good feeling causes an expansion, like a puffing out of the chest. (Such generalizations invite exceptions, but they provide a place to work from.)

The exercise is in three parts. The first two parts are separate exercises, each fully completed for its own value. The third part completes the entire exercise, using the first two parts in tandem.

An Exercise to Habituate Extremes of Feeling

Part One: Contraction

1. Stand in a neutral, relaxed, but attentive position.
2. Recall a painful feeling of your own.
3. Breathe the feeling in until it becomes so intense as to be felt throughout the body. (See a fuller version of filling the body with feeling in the next chapter's exercise.)
4. Imagine the pit of the stomach as the center of the body's gravity.

5. In your mind (not out loud) repeat the mantra, "I am so small, I am so small." (Repeat the mantra throughout the exercise.)

6. Imagine that the center of the feeling is in the pit of the stomach.

7. Imagine the feeling in the pit of the stomach as the center of gravity.

Imagine that the center draws all the energy of the feeling from the rest of the body, contracting it into the pit of the stomach until the painful feeling exists only in the pit of the stomach and you feel so small as to be nearly nonexistent.

Don't command the body to contract. The mantra of "I am so small" will direct the energy of the feeling to the pit of the stomach. There should only be a slight contraction, possibly a slight lowering of the head and a concave droop to the shoulders. Any more than that will compel a need to move. The purpose is to exercise the body's *intuitive capacity* for extreme feeling by concentrating the energy of it in the pit of the stomach.

8. Repeat the exercise in its entirety until it starts to feel habitual.

Part Two: Expansion

1. After a brief break, return to a neutral, relaxed, but attentive position.

2. Recall a joyous feeling.

3. Breathe feeling in until it becomes so intense as to be felt throughout the body.

4. In your mind (not out loud) repeat the mantra, "I am so large, I am so large." (Repeat the mantra throughout the exercise.)

5. Imagine a small ball of light in the center of the chest.

6. Still repeating the mantra, "I am so large, I am so large," allow the mind to direct the energy of the feeling into the ball of light until it pulsates with the energy.

7. Slowly spread your arms out horizontally, palms facing outward as you imagine the energy of the light spreading out horizontally from the center of the chest.

Let it spread through the arms and out the fingertips, past the confines of the space, until you feel the urge to extend the thought mantra to "I am so large, I am so large, I can hold this room from the outside."

8. Stay in this position, repeating the mantra.

Hold the position until the body realizes the full intensity of the feeling.

9. Repeat the exercise in its entirety until it feels habitual.

Part Three: Alternate Contraction and Expansion

1. Alternate contracting down into "I am so small" and expanding out into "I am so large" over and over, one after the other.

Repetition will embody a working dynamic of contraction and expansion between extremities of feeling.

The Line Exercise and this one, simple and economical as they are, are the foundation for all other exercise work.

Having sharpened a keen power of observation, habituated the body to the value of each moment, and exercised a readiness for extremes of feeling, the actor is prepared to take on the shape and behavior of a character's body.

4.
The Life Passion as Source of Character Behavior

Context

Before we get to the exercises related to feeling and body behavior, I'd like to take a moment to note a slight but important semantic confusion.

"Instinct" and "passion" are two words often used interchangeably. But conflating their meaning can be confusing. Like passion and thought process—working in time within time to create emotional behavior—we can make a distinction between passion and instinct for acting purposes. Let's start to clarify the distinction with a recap of what we know about the passion of suffering and the passion to survive.

Recall that every feeling response is first a dual embryonic biochemical interplay between a passion of suffering and a passion to survive it—an interplay that is the ontological source of all spontaneous behavior. In our look at instinctive and learned behavior, we considered the passion of suffering as a reactive state and the passion to survive as an act to ease that suffering. To begin that fundamental behavior, the brain instinctively releases chemicals from the adrenal glands to warn the body it is suffering a passionate *reaction* which, in an immeasurable but distinct time, creates an instinct in the mind to take a passionate *action*. In other words, the brain affects the body before the mind recognizes what to do with it.

If a passion of suffering is the root source of *instinctive* behavior, and a passion to survive is the source of *learned* behavior that prompts the instinctive need to act, it follows that a passion of suffering is the universal, root source of *spontaneous* behavior.

Merging life passions

The writer Wendell Berry refers to "the law that marries all things" as the means to engage that which is beyond comprehension. For Berry, music is the truest expression of that law.

For the art of acting, the truest expression of Berry's notion is the marriage of actor and character. The challenge, of course, is that the union of these two different persons is literal as well as figurative. The upcoming exercises are designed to make the figurative literal, or as Peter Brook says, to make visible the invisible

By the time actor and character are introduced by the play, they have lived different lives and have experienced separate passions, thought processes, and feelings that (excepting certain coincidental experiences) have made the differences between them. Consequently, there's a limit to how conscious an actor can be of all the experiences that both their lives bring to the play. The first job then is to find the common bond of attraction that inspires them to become one person.

However much their bond may lie beyond conscious comprehension, the merged presence of actor and character is a felt reality inspired by sharing a passion to survive in response to a passion of suffering. Actor and character are motivated to join forces because of an ever-present, ever-evolving basic human activity, a common bond that we are all one in the song of human suffering—that love is lost, that the tax collector will call, and that Dr. Death lies a-waiting in the wings.

There can be no truly spontaneous tragic or comic performance unless it is energized in response to a passion of suffering: no shamefully barren Yerma but that her marriage had been arranged to a man who didn't want children; no Oedipus the King but that, in the rash arrogance of youth, he slew a stranger on the road; no prisoner of Second Avenue without a burglary; no Viola without a shipwreck; and no

Queen Gertrude but that she bedded down with her husband's brother.

Let's see how an actor playing Gertrude uses exercise to effect the merger that makes this marriage between actor and character a felt reality.

The actor hasn't slept well the night after the first readthrough rehearsal of *Hamlet*. She awakens the next morning with an exhilarating but frustratingly inarticulate feeling that the psychic content of her life has been profoundly rearranged. As she's peeling a boiled egg for her breakfast, the feeling returns and gives her a sense something special happened in the closet scene in yesterday's rehearsal. It doesn't last long. Her irritation at having overcooked the egg has replaced any feeling of the sense of "inspiration" she'd felt upon awakening. She worries that today will be a bad day—one of those rehearsals when you're merely serviceable, not quite there. But she tells herself not to worry, it's only the second rehearsal.

Later, at today's rehearsal, the actor playing Gertrude feels a tremble—not quite conscious, but definite—as she reads the phrase "such black and grained spots" in the closet scene. Aha! She recognizes the intuitive response: that's the feeling she woke up with this morning! Having identified the source, she's ready to go to work.

The actor knows from experience that when the same intuitive response insists itself by repetition, it's most often a genuine clue to characterization. She knows those "black and grained spots" are a symptom of the passions that drove Gertrude, wittingly or unwittingly, to be Claudius's lover and accomplice to the murder of her husband, the king. She knows this tremble, this little nudge of something she's felt just now in rehearsal and this morning when she awakened, is where she'll find her connection to the life passion of Gertrude's suffering.

After the discovery in today's rehearsal, the actor playing Gertrude will exercise the merging of her life suffering with Gertrude's to ensure those "black and grained spots" remain the inspirational source for all Gertrude's external behavior.

The exercises in this and the next two sections are variations influenced mostly by Michael Chekov's work on the radiation of feeling and the psychology of gesture. They are intended as a step-by-step way to create muscle memory for a *body within the actor's body as an energetic source for a character's physical behavior.*

Here's the first exercise in that task.

While this exercise is being used here specifically to embody the character's passion of suffering, it can be used to reduce any feeling to its essential passion.

A caution: some actors become emotionally upset in the early stages of this exercise because of its feeling intensity. Any breath of free association might understandably cause some psychological trembling. Treat a psychic muscle in the same way you would treat a body muscle: take a break before pushing it too far and stretch it a little further the next try.

In this first exercise note that words should be thoughts, not spoken aloud. Also, the term *mandala* will be used to describe a visual stimulus for concentration and *mantra* used to describe an aural stimulus to concentration.

An Exercise to Embody Passion

Part One: Find a mantra and/or mandala

1. Revisit a beat in the scene.

The word "beat" has nearly as many definitions as there are practitioners of theatre. I'll offer you one that has proven most effective in my experience. A beat occurs whenever there is a sufficiently strong change of thought and/or feeling.

To begin the exercise, the actor playing Gertrude revisits the beat in Act III, Scene 4, the closet scene, when Queen Gertrude responds to Prince Hamlet's attempt to shame his mother for sharing bed and body with his uncle by saying:

O Hamlet, speak no more.
Thou turn'st my eyes into my very soul
And there I see such black and grained spots
As will not leave their tinct.

2. Use one's own language.

Using her own language to connect more immediately to the feeling condition in the beat, the actor refers to the feeling as "anguish." The actor's language, naturally, brings with it her own emotional associations, which intensify the feeling. She wants this. She wants to carry as much of her own like experience to Gertrude's feeling condition as she can.

3. Locate the telling phrase.

Once she feels an emotional kinship with the character, the actor playing Gertrude looks to find a telling phrase in the play that best expresses the character Gertrude's language for the feeling condition.

There's no rule for finding the right phrase to serve as a mantra for the exercise save to trust one's intuition. There's no logic to explain why, for this particular actor playing Gertrude, "such black and grained spots" serves as her mantra. It could just as well have been "speak no more."

4. Repeat the mantra.

Once she finds the mantra, the actor repeats it over and over, all the while feeling the emotional condition she first called "anguish," until she experiences a feeling condition which is the combined vocabularies of herself and Gertrude married into one mantra: a condition which is both autobiographical and imaginative.

This is where the exercise starts to become difficult. The actor is likely to become impatient because any vibrant feeling creates a desire to act upon it. But any impulse to action would be premature at this point because the actor's objective is to reduce feeling to its primitive passion of suffering. She wants not to act anything out but to *absorb any impulses to act into the feeling*. She needs to remind herself that she's not yet looking for the character, she's looking to give herself over to the *source* of character. By an act of will, she'll suppress the impulse to act on her feeling, because her goal is to enter that state of being which is a passion of suffering.

5. Breathe in the feeling.

The actor is ready to shift her attention to the simple, mechanical activity of breathing. Concentrating solely on the physical life of breathing and hypnotically repeating the thought *such black and grained spots* will empty her mind of all but a phenomenal awareness of the feeling.

6. Free associate.

Once in this singular feeling state, the actor continues to breathe in and out from her mantra as she free associates. Usually, the associations will inspire a series of visual images to serve as mandalas and/or a series of sounds to serve as mantras. She free associates until she intuitively senses when one of the associations is more appropriate to Gertrude's "black and grained spots."

The associations will occur to her in some combination of three ways: (1) observed, (2) autobiographical, and (3) imaginative. Say the actor recalls, among other associations, (1) the photo sequence from the Berliner Ensemble production of *Mother Courage* depicting Helene Weigel fainting at the news of her son's death, and (2) a phone call she herself received some while back, informing her that her son had been in a serious accident. She also visualizes, for no apparent reason, (3) a wounded bird trying to take flight.

At this point in the exercise, the actor might be tempted to act upon any one of her tangential scenarios. The experiences should not be denied but the impulse to act upon them should be rejected. If the wounded bird, for example, reminds the actor that she once got a bad notice in *The Seagull,* she should reject an impulse to plot revenge on a certain critic.

While working this exercise, it's best to stand in a neutral, relaxed position to eliminate any risk that a physical posture which expresses the actor's own personality will cause another distracting scenario. These tangential explorations are of great value to an actor in other ways we'll investigate later. But in this exercise, such tangents should be resisted because they take away from the business at hand, which is *to absorb her free associations until she finds a new mandala and/or mantra* as a means to embody in muscle memory a passion of suffering that is both actor's and character's.

Say, at some point, the telephone call informing her of her son's accident occurs in her mind as swirling images of shattered glass and mangled steel that will serve as a visual focus, a mandala. Say that, at the same time, she hears hundreds of voices murmuring a muffled sorrow. The actor's free association has inspired a new mandala/mantra of sight and sound, a surreal symbol, to begin to marry her own passion of suffering to Gertrude's.

7. Find the most intense connection.

The actor continues to free associate from the new mandala/mantra until she conjures the image of her son's accident-battered face—an image that intensifies the feeling to such a degree the actor intuits she's found the deepest connection to Gertrude's black and grained spots.

8. Transform the personal.

To prevent the literal image of her son's damaged face from creating an impulse to wander into the story of her own life, the actor continues to free associate. She's looking for a mandala and/or mantra that will transform her feeling of suffering to Gertrude's. She concentrates on a detail of her son's face, the downward turn of his once-smiling mouth— which calls up a succession of surreal symbols: an open grave, the vacuum and crackle of hell's fire, and an opaque, gray, endless atmosphere through which nothing can be seen.

For reasons she can't explain, but simply because she's here today, doing the exercise at this moment, the actor finds herself especially responsive to the visual image of an endless gray atmosphere.

She's ready for the heart of the exercise: to use the new mandala to embody the newly experienced feeling as the single combined passion of her and Gertrude's suffering.

Part Two: Embodiment

1. Focus on the image.

The actor devotes her attention completely and exclusively to the visual image. Once again, she concentrates on her breathing. She breathes in feeling from the image of endless gray, and breathes out more feeling into the image, to breathe in even more of its feeling. She keeps this up until all other considerations are absorbed by her concentration on the visual image of endless gray, until nothing else exists for her but the image and the new unnamable feeling it gives her. However, the feeling is not yet fully reduced to the passion that motivated it.

As described earlier, a passionate response is an "overwhelming, utterly singular reaction to a stimulus." The actor is ready to use the mandala—the opaque, endless gray image—as the stimulus to absorb the feeling until it fills her entire body with the utterly singular passion of Gertrude's suffering.

2. Find the source in the body.

Next, she looks for how the feeling is already affecting her body, usually in one or more of four places: head, throat, chest, stomach. These are the primary local stops for the feeling condition on its way to its main destination: the actor's entire, head-to-toe animal being. The feeling may first be felt in the head, behind the eyes, because the actor's concentration has been focused on the image. It could get stuck in her throat, as if she has difficulty "swallowing" the feeling. It may heat up her heart if she's sentimentalizing it. Or her stomach might be queasy if the feeling upsets her.

The psychology of the well-trained actor is almost always in some way connected to the character's psychology, and specific localities of feeling in the actor's body are symptoms of character behavior. Say the actor playing Gertrude experiences the feeling in her heart and chest. She makes note of it for later use. On reflection, she might interpret her overheated heart as symptomatic of the private needs of a public queen for a forbidden love, which could lead to some interesting interpretive choices such as intermittent flashes of fever. But that's for later.

3. Breathe in from the mandala into the affected part of the body.

For now, the actor focuses on breathing from the mandala directly to that area of her body most affected by the feeling. The actor playing Gertrude experiences the feeling in her chest as she breathes it in. She keeps breathing into her chest until the feeling becomes so intense it needs more living space. Then she moves on to the final stages of the exercise.

4. Breathe the feeling condition into the whole body.

The actor now concentrates on breathing all the energy of the feeling condition into her entire body. She's going to work her feeling out from heart and chest to fill her entire body with it. She imagines that each breath in fills up first her torso, then her arms and legs, then her head, and so forth, until each additional breath in from the mandala eventually fills her entire body, head to toe. The actor has made herself *subject to the external force* of the endless gray mandala, as in the Oxford definition of passion noted in Chapter 2.

While it's helpful, and probably necessary, to think of the exercise as "filling up" the body with passion, it's arguably more physiologically accurate to say one breathes passion into the bloodstream as textured oxygen. There's no simple definition that describes the feeling property of a breath of passion but—absent such a wonder—we nevertheless do recognize the magical substance of blood passion in idiomatic expressions: the blood runs thick with confusion, we say, or cold with fear or hot with love, and so on.

5. Habituate the presence of the passion.

Finally, the actor wants to work random moments in the play while she is filled with what is now a passion of suffering—a passion that is uniquely one and the same for actor and character. She'll do this not for interpretive purposes but until she can feel her muscle memory record the passion as the essential source of all Gertrude's past and present behavior.

6. Repeat the above to create more connections.

Given that day-to-day experiences will cause minute, unconscious shifts of feeling emphases, there may be times when an actor loses the connection. Other associations can serve equally well by creating other images and sounds to stimulate the merging passions of actor and character. For this reason, the exercise is best done many times to keep a package of stimuli at the ready.

Other uses

It's worth a reminder that an exercise is a dynamic process of craft to bring into actuality what the play has already inspired in the actor's imagination—an imagination that is already forming characterization. Therefore, the actor can use this step at any stage of the work, even before the first rehearsal, because she's been inspired by the play.

The exercise can also serve as a nearly foolproof preparation for performance that will ready the actor for the full range of Gertrude's feelings. She can use its images and/or sounds as a focus for the *I am so small* part of the Exercise to Habituate Extremes of Feeling. And she can use them to find a passion of joy to focus on in the *I am so large* part.

It can also be used as an aid to concentration in study or rehearsal. If, for instance, the actor playing Gertrude is worried about being distracted by a call from her daughter's college asking for payment, she can use the exercise to regain her focus.

One of the happier ways to use it is when things go awry in performance. Suppose the actor playing Gertrude forgets her line when she's distracted by a rather loud midwinter cough from somewhere in the middle of the house just as she's about to toast Hamlet prior to the duel with Laertes. If, in the pause before raising her glass, she makes a brief, conscious choice to breathe in the endless gray mandala she saw weeks ago in rehearsal, she'll be right back in character (without anyone realizing she'd gone up) and able to say, "The queen carouses to thy fortune, Hamlet," before she swallows the poisoned wine that will end her life.

By the conclusion of the exercise, the actor has begun the process of using muscle memory to affect external behavior—a process that is just the beginning of achieving a body *consistently* in character.

The next exercise deals with how to create an inner body that will become the source to motivate the character's external behavior.

5.
The Body Within

Context

Recall that Gertrude's passion of suffering is *reactive*, a suffering which creates an *active* response from an internalized universal passion to survive.

Both these responses are instinctive at birth. They remain invisible to the eye and become visible only when an *active* passion to survive creates emotional behavior in response to the *reactive* passion of suffering. That is to say, we know nothing about the inner life in the figure of a character until it is reflected in how the character moves, speaks, and gestures in response to events.

This basic internal and external activity coexists in the body. Every character in a play arrives *de facto* with a reactive body shaped by its past behavior which determines in great measure how its present *active body* will respond in the time of the play. Just as actors change their own thought processes in order to speak in character, so, too, do they use the muscle memories of a character's past behavior as instinctive body-thought to stimulate spontaneous movement and gesture in character.

This exercise is in four parts. The first two parts focus on incorporating the muscle memory of past behavior into the figure of the reactive body within. The third part is exercising how the reactive body within affects the active body in the present time of the play. The fourth part exercises how they work together in present time.

An Exercise for the Body Within

Part One: The Reactive Body as Source for the Active Body

1. Find a variation of the character's life suffering from a prior event in the play.

The actor looks for a moment early in the play when Gertrude is recognizably affected by the murder of her husband and her marriage to his brother. She finds it in Act I, Scene 2, when Gertrude urges Hamlet to accept his father's death and "cast thy knighted color off," which causes a lightning flash of hatred in Hamlet's eyes as he responds by saying "all that lives must die."

2. Use one's own language.

To connect her immediate self closely to Gertrude, the actor playing Gertrude refers to the feeling in her own language as "fear."

(Again, words should be *thoughts*, not spoken aloud. And again, *mandala* and/or *mantra* will be used to describe a visual and/or aural focus.)

3. Find the telling phrase.

Once she feels a kinship with the character, she uses Hamlet's phrase "all that lives must die" as a mantra for Gertrude's language to focus on the *phenomenon of the feeling* rather than a logical statement of it.

(Recall this mantra belongs to Gertrude's present-time passion of suffering in response to the murder before the play—a response caused by the hatred in her son's eyes.)

4. Repeat the mantra.

The actor repeats the phrase over and over, all the while feeling what she first called "fear," until she experiences a feeling condition which is the combined vocabularies of herself and Gertrude married into the one mantra—a condition both autobiographical and imagined.

5. Breathe in the feeling.

Next, she shifts her attention to the simple, mechanical activity of breathing. Her concentration is solely on the physical life of breathing while hypnotically repeating the thought "all that lives must die" to empty her mind of all but the phenomenal awareness of the feeling.

6. Free associate.

Now, she lets her mind wander in a free association of analogous ideas and experiences to intensify the feeling. For this exercise, the actor is specifically looking for a visual image to serve as a mandala because she's laying the groundwork for Gertrude's *physical behavior*. (A reminder not to use any associations that decrease the intensity of the feeling.) Say the actor recalls, with horror, Rubens' painting of the rape of Lucretia.

7. Embody the present-time passion of suffering.

Using the mandala of the painting, the actor repeats Steps 1 through 4 of Part Two: Embodiment from the Exercise to Embody Passion to fill her body with the present-time passion.

8. Focus on the image.

Once her body is in full passion, the actor devotes her attention completely and exclusively to the visual image. Once again, she concentrates on her breathing. She breathes in feeling from the image of the horrified Lucretia attempting to flee from her would-be rapist and breathes out more feeling into the image, to breathe in even more of its feeling. She keeps this up until all other considerations are absorbed by her concentration on the visual image of Lucretia reacting in horror until nothing else exists for her but the image of Lucretia's figure and the energy of the new unnamable feeling it gives her.

9. Find the source in the body.

Next, she determines how the present-time suffering is affecting her body. In the previous exercise to embody Gertrude's suffering, the actor located the feeling in her overheated heart and chest. This time, she locates the present-time suffering as a pain behind her eyes.

10. Breathe the feeling into the affected part of the body.

For now, the actor focuses on breathing the feeling from the figure of Lucretia directly to that area of her body most affected by it. She imagines the breath giving more life and substance to the feeling. She keeps breathing into the pain behind her eyes until the feeling becomes so intense it needs more living space. Then she moves on to the final stages of the exercise.

11. Breathe the feeling condition into the whole body.

The actor now concentrates on breathing all the energy of the newer feeling condition into her entire body. She's going to work her feeling out from behind her eyes to fill her entire body with it. She imagines that each breath in fills up first her head, then her torso, then her arms and legs, until each additional breath in from the mandala eventually fills her entire body, head to toe.

When Gertrude's life passion of suffering—as activated by the image of Lucretia—is fully incorporated in her present-time suffering, the actor is ready to internalize it as muscle memory.

Part Two: Internalizing the Reactive Body

1. Shift the focus.

While her body is filled with horrific passion, the actor closes her eyes and imagines, in *her mind's eye*, the line of a horizon in an empty space. The neutral, empty space will prevent other associations from affecting the objective of the exercise.

2. Find a still life portrait.

On the line of the horizon, the actor asks Gertrude to appear as the figure she saw in her mind's eye, Lucretia attempting to flee. Say the actor, looking at Gertrude in her mind's eye, sees her twisting away, as Lucretia does in the painting, her head looking back in horror, her legs locked together, her right arm extended to ward off her would-be rapist, her left arm holding fast what's left of her red garment to stop him from tearing it away and leaving her completely exposed to his violation.

The passion of horror filling the actor's body causes the figure of Lucretia to faint and collapse into a broken marionette. The broken marionette becomes the searched-for still life portrait.

3. Breathe in the feeling from the figure of the still life.

Now the actor concentrates on breathing the passion as affected by the horrified broken marionette *into her torso* to make more complete the connection between the figure and the image of it in her mind's eye. (Because the actor is looking for the active body as instinct for external behavior, it's important at this stage to confine the body focus to the torso only.)

4. Project the figure.

Once the connection is made, the actor *opens her eyes* for the first time and focuses on a place that can act as a neutral screen. She projects the figure of the marionette onto the horizon of empty space.

5. Copy the figure.

Then, still confining the feeling to her torso only, she copies with her body the figure of the broken marionette, being sure to duplicate it in complete detail.

6. Duplicate the muscular life.

Next, the actor duplicates the muscular life of the figure by releasing the feeling in her torso to the rest of her body, being mindful of how the feeling affects the muscular support of the figure's body. Occasionally, an actor might flash the complete muscular life of the figure all at once, but usually this part of the exercise requires perseverance.

7. Breathe the muscular life and the feeling into the torso.

Again, the actor concentrates her breathing, this time to draw both the feeling and the impressions of its muscular support from her extremities back into her torso. Once Gertrude's present-time passion of suffering in the play—the hatred in her son's eyes—becomes a feeling in the actor's torso, she then imagines that feeling as the figure of the broken marionette.

She has, in effect, given imaginative shape to a reactive body (the broken marionette) in her torso. The feeling is now a complete body within—a body pulsing with Gertrude's passionate desire to take an action to relieve her suffering.

Next, we turn to Parts Three and Four, which are perhaps the most difficult of the exercise. Having created an imaginative shape for the *reactive* body, the actor playing Gertrude will, in Part Three, create a different imaginative shape for the *active* body. In Part Four, she will internalize it as the active body within. By incorporating both bodies, the actor will be instinctively available to suffer a response and then do something about it.

Part Three: The Active Body

1. Find a present-time active objective.

To provide an objective for the active body to satisfy Gertrude's need to escape her suffering, the actor goes directly to the play for a moment that best expresses that objective. She finds it in Act V, Scene 1, when Gertrude, in her sorrow, says "I hoped thou shouldst have been my Hamlet's wife" as she strews flowers over Ophelia's grave.

2. Return to the reactive body within.

The actor begins by bringing the shape of the broken marionette back into her torso. The purpose is to ensure that its suffering is absorbed into her body to provide instinctive motivation for the active body she is about to discover. (The actor may or may not have to repeat some or all of Part One: The Reactive Body.)

3. Find the telling phrase.

Once in the feeling activated by the broken marionette, she places herself in the feeling condition of the moment over Ophelia's grave and from Gertrude's line *thou shouldst have been my Hamlet's wife,* she uses the phrase *my Hamlet's wife* as a mantra. (Again, words should be thoughts, not spoken aloud. And again, mandala and/or mantra will be used to describe a visual and/or aural focus.)

4. Breathe in the feeling.

Next, the actor shifts her attention to the simple, mechanical activity of breathing, concentrating solely on the act of breathing as she hypnotically repeats the new mantra to empty her mind of all but a phenomenal awareness of the feeling.

5. Free associate.

The actor is in search of an active body that will motivate her need for the objective to survive the present-time horror of Gertrude's life. Therefore, she's directing her associations toward an imagined positive time. She lets her mind wander in a free association of analogous ideas and experiences to intensify the desire to survive. (A reminder not to use any associations that decrease the intensity of the feeling.)

Say she imagines a portrait of Gertrude as Queen Mother raising a joyful toast at a feast to the cheers of hundreds upon the birth of a male heir from the marriage of Hamlet and Ophelia.

(Notice how this association is pregnant with potential action because it contains both past and future in the need of the present moment: *past* in the shape of a life's joy she had anticipated before the troubles of the play and a *future* suggested by the fateful raising of the glass.)

6. Breathe in the active feeling of the figure in the portrait.

Now the actor concentrates on breathing the joy of the portrait of the joyful figure of the raised toast into her torso to *replace* the suffering of the horrified broken marionette.

(Because the actor is creating the active body as instinct for external behavior, it's important to confine the body focus to the torso only.)

7. Project the figure.

Once the connection is made, the actor focuses on a place that can act as a neutral screen. She projects the figure of the raised toast onto the horizon of an empty space.

8. Copy the figure.

Then, confining the feeling to her torso only, she copies with her body the figure of the joyful queen raising a toast, being sure to duplicate every detail.

9. Duplicate the muscular life.

Next, the actor duplicates the muscular life of the figure by releasing the feeling in her torso to the rest of her body, being mindful of how the feeling affects the muscular support of the figure's body. Occasionally, an actor might flash the complete muscular life of the image all at once, but usually this part of the exercise requires perseverance.

10. Breathe the muscular life and the feeling into the torso.

Again, the actor concentrates her breathing, this time to draw both the feeling of joy and the impressions of its muscular support from her extremities back into her torso. Then the actor imagines the feeling in her torso as the figure of the joyful Queen Mother raising a toast.

11. Habituate the presence of the active body.

The actor works random moments in the play to connect the imagined active body within her torso to affect Gertrude's behavior. She chooses random moments not for interpretive purposes but to get the feel of how the subtextual history of Gertrude's passion for joy affects the behavior of her active body.

Part Four: Absorb the Reactive Body into the Active Body

1. Breathe in the shape of the reactive body.

While she remains in the joyful feeling of the toasting queen in her torso, she breathes the shape of the broken marionette with its horrific suffering into her torso. The purpose is not to eliminate the shape of the joyful queen in her torso but to *have it absorbed as pentimento, a presence painted over by the active body.*

By the time the actor playing Gertrude has finished the four parts of the exercise in sequence, she will have made a subtle but significant change in her own body. She will, in effect, have internalized Gertrude's muscle memory into her body as a living presence of the character's dual instincts to *react* with a passion of suffering and *act* from a passion to survive it. Gertrude's external expressions of her feeling behavior in present time will be the natural, spontaneous result of her past.

Putting the active body to use

Here's a sequence from the closet scene to illustrate how Gertrude's behavior (past and present) might spontaneously manifest in the body in rehearsal.

When Gertrude hears Hamlet calling "Mother, mother, mother," for a brief moment she feels her body wanting to collapse *like a marionette whose strings have been cut,* but she quickly takes command of herself by *raising her head high with the back of her left hand as if it were pulled up by a marionette string.*

And when Hamlet pleads for his mother to see the ghost of his father, Gertrude suffers a brief flash of the *first mandala of endless gray* (the symptom of the hatred in Hamlet's eyes), and is so overwhelmed with horror and suffering that she immediately experiences a brief flash of Rubens' painting of Lucretia—body twisting away, head looking back in horror—a flash that causes Gertrude to unconsciously *twist her own body away* from Hamlet in horror.

Later in the scene, as she says, "O, Hamlet thou hast cleft my heart in twain," in response to his plea for her to refrain from going to his uncle's bed, she *raises her arm in half-reach* to beseech his understanding—a gesture instinctively prompted by *the raised-arm toast of joy* the actor found in exercise.

The actor has successfully incorporated a body within shaped by the character's past behavior.

You may notice that all the exercises for preparing the actor's body, thus far, have their foundation in An Exercise to Habituate Extremes of Feeling. And, like the previous exercises, this one can be used as preparation for rehearsal and/or performance as a way to get back in character from a break in concentration.

The next two sections will exercise how the inner body assures spontaneous character behavior. The first section illustrates how to create instinctive lifelong character habits, the second how to create instinctive learned character habits.

6.
Instinctive Habits

Context

We've just seen the actor characterize the active body, with its instinct to survive, as the body within Gertrude and use that instinct to create character behavior.

In the upcoming exercise, the actor playing Gertrude will discover certain gestures and/or movements from the work she has already done up to this point in rehearsals. She will then exercise to incorporate them as Gertrude's *lifelong habits of instinctive behavior.* This will assure all her interpretive choices—habitual and occasional—are played spontaneously.

The interpretive groundwork

Shakespeare leaves the question of Gertrude's complicity in the murder of Hamlet's father open to interpretation. Were both of her marriages to satisfy ambition? Did she suffer erotic frustration in her marriage to Hamlet's father? Is that her attraction to Claudius? Is she a thrill-seeker? Did she love either of her two husbands? Or does she in fact, still, love them both? What does Gertrude know, and what doesn't she know? For the actor, the answer to the question of whether Gertrude's death is accidental or a conscious choice is basic to making choices for a cohesive interpretation of Gertrude.

The actor is certain of one thing: she'll not play Gertrude as—God forbid—she saw her played one time: empty-headed and oblivious to the very end. For that reason, she chooses to play Gertrude's drinking of the poison as a conscious choice. Now the actor has to create a case for her interpretation by establishing a version of the murder of her husband that happened prior to the play.

It seems clear to the actor playing Gertrude that, in Act I, Scene 4, the Ghost of Hamlet's Father believes Claudius has inspired lust in the king's previously virtuous wife. She also notes that the Ghost tells Hamlet not to contrive against his mother but to "Leave her to Heaven / And to those thorns that in her bosom lodge / To prick and sting her." The lines suggest Gertrude is willfully blind to her complicity in the murder.

The actor imagines a scene in which Gertrude tells Claudius she feels guilty for betraying her husband. Claudius, fearful he might lose her, says aloud he cannot give her up and he wishes the king were dead so they could marry. Gertrude, moved by the intensity of a love she has always needed—a love without bounds—cannot bring herself to believe Claudius really means what he says.

Since, in the actor's interpretation, Gertrude was not present at the killing, she'll need to imagine a second scenario in which she experiences the denial of the murder—a denial already made possible by Gertrude's unconscious misreading of Claudius's intent. Gertrude reacts with stunned horror when Claudius tells her he has killed the king for his love of her. Given the raging conflict of her guilt and her passion for Claudius, and the fact she has nowhere to turn. In the scenario, she sees a flash of those "dark and grained spots," feels herself faint, as if the marionette strings have been cut, and falls into Claudius's arms to accept the comfort of his love and obliterate any conscious memory of the murder.

Next, the actor looks for a critical moment that awakens Gertrude to her complicity. She finds it when Gertrude frames her answer to Hamlet's accusation that Claudius murdered the king in the form of a question, "As kill a King?" She plans to play the moment as a significant crack in a badly constructed dam of denial from which a torrent of self-recrimination will eventually pour forth, leading to the tragedy of her death.

Preparation for the exercise

Acknowledging that DNA can be host to a genetic predisposition toward potential life-threatening disease(s), the actor will choose and exercise an illness appropriate to Gertrude's subconscious need for survival. Then she will exercise the symptoms of the illness. From those symptoms, she will create life habits of Gertrude's behavior.

Her interpretation has led her to make her choice from Gertrude's line, said with poisoned chalice raised, "The queen *carouses* to thy fortune, Hamlet." (Italics mine.) She interprets the word choice as Gertrude's horrific recognition of the truth at last. She's been playing the moment with a nearly deranged mixture of grief, bitter irony, guilt, motherly love, rage, and thrill of sacrifice.

It's true that the symptoms of Gertrude's illness are brought on by poison not an organic disease. But the actual cause of a character's death is not what is under consideration in the exercise. The actor's concern here is the *symptoms of potential illness inherent in a character's body*: symptoms from which to create life habits of character behavior.

An Exercise for Instinctive Life Habits

1. Locate the active shape of suffering.

The actor playing Gertrude returns to the active shape of suffering and its feeling—the body twisting away and looking back in horror.

2. Find an illness as metaphor.

Next, she imagines an illness that will serve as a metaphor for the body's feeling condition. Sometimes it comes in a flash of inspiration, but more often it's found by trial and error. In this instance, Shakespeare has given her death by poison.

Claudius committed the crime of killing his brother with a toxic overdose of hebenon (commonly called "henbane") poured into the ear of the sleeping king. Since Gertrude's denial of the murder is a primary source of her inner conflict in the play, death by poison seems appropriate.

3. Study the illness.

The next step is to study the illness. The actor playing Gertrude is looking for two things: (1) the bodily expressions of symptoms and (2) the bodily expressions of living with and treating the illness. (Note how the activity is parallel to the reactive and active bodies within.) The research should be as thorough as if the play were, in fact, about the character suffering the illness.

Here's some of what she finds: side effects of poison can include hallucinations, dilated pupils, restlessness, flushed skin, convulsions, vomiting, hypertension, dryness in the mouth, confusion, locomotor and memory disturbances. Large doses can cause delirium, coma, respiratory paralysis, and death. Low and average dosages can have inebriating and aphrodisiac effects.

4. Choose symptoms of behavior.

The actor picks a few symptoms of death by poison she thinks appropriate for use as gestural behavior that would reflect Gertrude's guilt. (As always when dealing with the literalness and academic thoroughness of research, the actor needs to trust intuition as well as reason in the choice of symptoms for the often-inexplicable interplay of paradox, ambiguity, pathology, and virtue in a character.)

Hypertension might manifest as headache, respiratory failure as throat constriction and brief stoppages of breath, paralysis as a momentary delay in committing an action or even a freeze during action. The low-dosage effects of inebriation and aphrodisia could serve as symptoms of self-treatment: an affection for wine that suggests an occasional slurring of a word or two and a frequent need to touch Claudius.

For instance, every now and then, at random, Gertrude might put two fingers to her right temple to ward off a phantom headache (symptom of hypertension). Or the actor might interpret Gertrude as so stunned after gasping in the truth of Claudius's murder of the king that she cannot move or breathe out (symptoms of respiratory failure and paralysis) for some seconds before she can ask, "As kill a king?" The scene becomes, in effect, a death scene—melodramatic, operatic in its execution.

5. Choose the critical beat in the scene.

The actor chooses the beat in the closet scene when Hamlet accuses Claudius of the "rash and bloody" killing of a king as the critical beat that cracks the surface of Gertrude's denial.

6. Play the beat as melodrama. She will *play the beat as if Gertrude suffers a potentially fatal attack of the illness,* working in all the chosen symptoms, while trying to achieve her intention to deny her guilt.

7. Play the beat in context. Without conscious attempt to employ the gestures, she plays the beat in context while she remembers the beat as melodrama. This will prime the body to activate the unconscious psychosomatic stresses and create muscle memory of instinctive habits.

8. Work the gestures.

The actor works the gestures in two ways: (1) *indiscriminately*, at random, throughout the play, to exercise the unconscious habit of the gesture, and (2) *at selected moments* for interpretive purposes.

9. Repeat to habituate behavior.

In the Exercise for the Body Within, the actor made a history of instinctive behavior manifest in the combined muscle memories of the reactive figure of the marionette and the active figure raising a toast. She then used illness in this exercise to create external behavior appropriate to her interpretation of Gertrude.

What began as a barely noticeable tremor of connection, inspired by the phrase "I see such black and grained spots" will now, in a nanosecond of instinct, activate each of Gertrude's spontaneous movements and gestures of habitual life behavior.

Let's give the actor playing Gertrude a well-deserved break and ask the actor playing Vershinin in *Three Sisters* to illustrate an exercise that uses the muscle memory of an instinctive need to survive to create learned habits of movement and gesture.

7.
Learned Habits

Context

As we saw with the actor playing Gertrude, instinctive lifelong gestural habits of behavior are an essential part of being in character. Those gestures are motivated by an instinctive passion to survive. In the upcoming exercise, the actor playing Vershinin will seek out gestures that, in addition, best express the essence of the character in present time—learned gestures that have become habitually ingrained as experiential attempts at survival.

The exercise makes significant use of Stanislavski's historic articulation of sense memory, which arguably may be the single most important tool an actor has to embody the life of the imagination. Conscious memory alone can easily fall victim to a limited, biased, opinionated view of experience. The complete experience of a recollected or imagined scene can only be absorbed into body memory if it is touched, heard, seen, tasted, or smelled.

Sense memory and substitution

Before we go on to the exercise, I'd like to briefly address the unnecessary but persistent question about the validity of using personal experience in characterization, a practice often called substitution.

As we've seen throughout the work to this point, the goal is to effect a merger of actor and character. And since an actor is *de facto* present, personal experiences are present as well.

There are three ways to use personal experience in characterization: improvisational as a means of finding a feeling kinship with character; improvisational in collaboration with a playwright to enhance or develop a character's behavior; and, lastly, as personal substitution on the occasion when an actor's personal experience is coincidentally appropriate to interpretation of character.

Substitution is one of the significant angles an actor uses to hold the "mirror up to nature." When used with discretion, it is integral to a personal interpretation.

An Exercise for Learned Character Habits

Part One: Creating Past Habit

A successful professional poker player sizes up their fellow gamblers by looking for tics or mannerisms that betray their mental and emotional states. In the poker business this is called looking for the "tell." So, too, an actor looks for the tell(s) in a character's behavior.

1. Find an essential habit of behavior. It's axiomatic that the more often a character behaves in a certain way, the more deeply ingrained is the habit of behavior.

The fact that the character philosophizes at seven different times in the play convinces the actor playing Vershinin that the character's most noticeable tell is his habit of talking too much; he will, unprompted, philosophize at length on the fate of the world and the Russian character.

Even before Vershinin's arrival in the play, Tuzenbach informs the sisters that Vershinin "talks a lot." And so true it is. He's hardly introduced himself before he's off on a tangent, and throughout the play he carries on at the slightest provocation. Vershinin's habit of philosophizing is so habitual that, in Act III—despite the fact it's deep into a night when a tragic fire might have destroyed the town, and, ironically, his exhausted, despairing audience has fallen asleep—he continues to rhapsodize about a glorious future. Even at the end of the play, about to embark on his march to obscurity, heartbroken to leave Masha, he will, gallant and foolish, attempt to philosophize his way from despair to his hope for a better world. His attempt to keep hope alive in the midst of despair is also what makes him a sympathetic character—comic and tragic at the same time.

2. Choose a moment in the scene when the character's need for the telling gesture is urgent. (For acting purposes, speaking can be considered a gestural act.)

Vershinin sits in the reception parlor of the three Prozorov sisters' house waiting for the servant Anfisa to serve the tea he's asked for. He hasn't eaten all day. This morning his mentally troubled wife railed at him in front of the children. His impulsive confession of love for Masha, who's unfortunately married to the local schoolteacher, has just been interrupted by the arrival of Masha's sister, Irina, and her hopeless suitor, Baron Tuzenbach, a lieutenant under Vershinin's command. Irina has just complained of being tired and disillusioned with working in the telegraph office. Brother Andrey is gambling away the household money. Chebutykin, the alcoholic eccentric army doctor who never married because he had loved the sisters' mother, has seated himself in the adjoining dining room to comb his beard and read the newspaper. He asks Irina to join him for a game of cards. There's a moment's silence. Still no tea has been served.

Vershinin, heart bursting with love for Masha, frustrated, impatient, and thirsty for tea, is moved to philosophize.

3. Find a motive from the character's past.

Is Vershinin afraid that in his despair he'll go public and let the cat out of the bag by declaring himself for Masha? Is he attempting to escape the memory of a near nervous breakdown during military training? Is he trying to shut out the vision of an incontinent old age? Is he trying to impress the others he is a civilized man, worthy of Masha's love? Does he imagine reading Pushkin with Masha? Is he recalling that a fellow reader once invited him to a Paris salon? Is he cynically trying to make fools of the others because he's convinced they think *him* a fool? Is he remembering an admired teacher who loved the Greeks? Is he simply trying to cover up a growling stomach in company?

From his imaginative wandering through many of Vershinin's possible motivations, a certain episode from Vershinin's past will seem like a possible habit for this moment in the dining room to distract himself from an uncomfortable feeling.

The actor's personal experiences are likely to be part of these imaginative wanderings. They are not helpful at this early stage of the exercise, but the actor should recognize them and save them for later.

4. Imagine character's past experience.

Suppose the actor imagines Vershinin, a young brigadier in search of promotion to Brigade Major, sitting in a Moscow barracks some years ago anxiously awaiting a response from his commanding officer to his paper on the artillery tactics of the Franco-Prussian War. Suppose, further, the actor imagines Vershinin, to ease his anxiety, shares a bottle of vodka with Mikhail, a fellow brigadier, while reading aloud from Jules Verne's *Twenty Thousand Leagues Under the Sea.*

Notice the imagined past experience does not directly mirror Vershinin's habit of philosophizing. It need only be a like circumstance to that which causes Vershinin to philosophize in the present time of the play. The actor is not bound by interpretation of character here. Some of the work will be valuable to interpretation, some will not. Some will even seem contradictory to an interpretation. But all of it, without exception, will eventually contribute to the resonant *presence* of the character.

5. Create detail.

The actor proceeds to create, in fine detail, the particulars of the scene: time of day, season, what Mikhail looks like, where the vodka came from, whether they're alone in the barracks, and so on.

6. Find the signature moment in the scene.

Once the scene is fully detailed, the actor runs it like a movie in his mind. He's looking for a signature moment that gives him a feeling strong enough to capture the life of the whole scene. Suppose the connection happens when Mikhail suddenly bursts out laughing at how drunk Vershinin is, and the woozy Vershinin finds himself laughing along with his equally tipsy comrade.

7. Freezeframe the moment.

Now the actor freezes the moment in his mind. Freezeframing the moment is important because he's looking for the *experience* of the imagined scene and not his *interpretation* of it by way of narrative summary. (A bit later we'll deal with how to use personal experience in the same way.)

8. Find sense memories.

The actor focuses on the freezeframed moment, breathing in the phenomenon of the feeling itself, until he finds a sensory experience connected to the moment. Say, in that shared moment of tipsy laughter with Mikhail, Vershinin has broken free, distracted himself from the anxiety of having to pass muster with the army. Say further that all the history of Vershinin's need to distract himself from uncomfortable situations is echoed in his sense memory of their tipsy laughter.

9. Breathe in the feeling from the sense memory.

The actor concentrates on breathing in the feeling of camaraderie from the sound of tipsy laughter to embody the feeling essence of the imagined scene. The sensory experience of hearing the tipsy laughter and the feeling of camaraderie associated with it will later be part of the wellspring of feeling that motivates Vershinin's habit of philosophizing.

10. Repeat.

The actor repeats Step 10 as often as necessary until he need only recall the sound of the tipsy laughter to bring back the feeling of the scene without having to reimagine it.

As is true throughout the work, *directed and concentrated breathing* is singularly necessary for effective exercise.

Part Two: Motivating Present with Past Habit

1. Exercise thought process.

Once the actor playing Vershinin can recall at will the feeling of delight in the imagined scene by hearing Mikhail's laughter, he then exercises it as a subtextual layer of Vershinin's thought process. He says the line "Well, if they won't give us tea, let us at least philosophize a little bit," prompted by the sensory sensation of tipsy laughter. He connects the feeling from sense memory of the imagined scene to the line from the play over and over until the sensation becomes, by second nature, an unspoken resonance of Vershinin's thought process. The actor has embodied a single imagined past experience as one of many sources for the character's telling habit of philosophizing.

2. Locate sensory detail in the present.

Next, the actor looks for a coincidental sensory experience in the circumstances of the play—an immediate sensory detail to motivate Vershinin's habit to philosophize spontaneously in the present.

Among the possibilities are the sound of Chebutykin's labored breathing interrupting the silence, the glow of the oil lamps, Tuzenbach's lovesick gaze at Irina as she lays out her playing cards, Masha's toe-tapping restlessness. He might become acutely aware of the sound of the cards as Irina slaps them on the table. He might think he hears the laughter of the buskers down the street.

Say the sound of Irina flapping the cards cues the sense memory of laughter and camaraderie with his comrade, Mikhail. The flapping cards might on the surface seem to make no sense. But the actor, trusting to his instinct, might discover a pleasing, oddly optimistic, nostalgia for a youth of better days in the presence of young Irina.

3. Breathe in sensory detail.

Now he exercises hearing the flapping of the cards as the sound of laughter. He then breathes in the sound of the cards again, and again, and over again, until the sound of the cards cues a nuance of optimistic nostalgia in Vershinin's impulse to philosophize.

Repetition is the key to success with the exercise. Whatever time it takes to exercise the past experience with Mikhail, whatever time it takes to exercise the sense memory of laughter and the feeling of camaraderie, whatever time it takes to transform laughter to the flapping of the cards is the time it takes.

4. Create more past experiences to find more sensory options.

At this point, the actor has accomplished the embodiment of but *one* in an uncountable number of past experiences that make up the history of Vershinin's habit of philosophizing. Besides actual incidents, Vershinin's experience also includes imagined flights of fancy, daydreams, night dreams, clairvoyant glimpses of the future, the constant conscious and unconscious absorption of culture and environment. The actor wants to give himself more options for possible motivations: perhaps Vershinin misremembers a tyrannical father as a loving parent, or he might once have abandoned a half-written novel, etcetera, etcetera.

The actor repeats the entire exercise to find as many options that will affect the subtextual nuances of the moment as possible. Numbers being arbitrary, if the actor finds five ways to motivate each of the seven times it happens in the play, he'll have found thirty-five essential motives true to Vershinin's habit of philosophizing: past experiences that give the actor intuitive options to be newly spontaneous eight times a week.

How the scene plays

At the next rehearsal after the successful completion of the exercise, the actor will find Vershinin charged with love for Masha while he's thinking he'd love a cup of tea. The flapping of Irina's cards in the present moment of silence will cue the subtextual laughter of twenty years past. In a flash, he imagines a civilized Utopia in the future as he sits in the second-floor apartment of the Prozorov house on a chair that squeaks a little, at eight o'clock of a chilly evening, waiting for the buskers to arrive to entertain, as is the custom for Carnival Week. He flashes a fancy of himself a member of the intelligentsia, a proud contributor to the French model of a bourgeois culture, unaware that the impending Russo-Japanese War will begin the historic downfall of the Tsar and lead to the Bolshevik Revolution. And the actor will embody all this as a simple impulse born of a lifetime's habit of philosophizing—because the tea is late!

Using personal experience

At the beginning of this section, I noted that substitutions of personal experience may be either appropriate or inappropriate to characterization. To illustrate the trial and error of the process, let's use the same moment of calling for the tea to look at an inappropriate substitution of personal experience.

The actor playing Vershinin is always on the lookout to find personal experiences that help make the part his own. He rummages through his memories in hope of finding something appropriate. He wonders if a personal experience would be helpful in the beat. If so, what will it be? A romance with a philosophy major in his undergraduate days? A favorite uncle who was fond of tea? A momentary regret that his father never saw him act? Admiration for his fellow actor's beard-combing business? Is he inspired by parallels between Shakespeare's Polonius and Vershinin? Is he anticipating that the director will ask him to pick up his cue? A thought he had too big a lunch today?

Say the actor substitutes his own personal habit of whiling away time by watching nature shows instead of using the sound of Mikhail's laughter in the Moscow barracks. Any number of things might happen to make this an inappropriate choice. His voice might betray a hint of a professional narrative tone rather than the more appropriate nuance of hopeful enthusiasm. He could feel he's sitting in his New York apartment rather than the Prozorov house in provincial Russia. TV images of an ecologically earnest naturalist in the Amazon rain forest are not likely to give nuance to Vershinin's feeling in quite the same way as a vision of a beaver-hatted Mikhail in a Moscow winter would do.

However, keep in mind nothing is lost in rehearsal. Any single detail of a personal experience may be coincident to the life of the character. A detail which is out of character in one moment may turn out to be useful in another. For instance, the actor may find the experience of pleasure he gets from making parallels between animal and human life can belong to Vershinin's vision of a Golden Age in the future.

Now, on to an appropriate substitution of personal experience.

When a personal experience insistently repeats itself, it's usually pointing the actor to an appropriate choice. Suppose the comradely laughter the actor imagined Vershinin sharing with another brigadier had occurred only one time in the exercise, but that three or four times the actor recalled a boyhood experience when an eight-year-old schoolgirl he had a crush on laughed gaily at a joke he told her. If instead of Vershinin's days as a brigadier, the actor chooses to interpret the schoolgirl's childhood laughter as Vershinin's wish to be innocent of the adulterous reality of his affair with Masha, the actor then would interpret Vershinin's willful innocence as a nuance for his need to philosophize.

Nonhabitual behavior

Every gesture in a performance is a micro expression of a life action which validates the character's presence.

Vershinin has, of course, other habits which, if not as habitual as his telling habit of philosophizing, contribute to the visual composition of his character. Such habits may be occasional to the play but not necessarily connected to the character's main action.

For example, at his first entrance, the contrast between the generous size of the Prozorov reception room with its profusion of flowers and his sparse and constantly moving military life might betray a habit of envy and longing for a better, more permanent life. The actor might then find interesting ways of expressing Vershinin's occasional covetousness, like lingering a bit too long over Masha's family ring when he takes her hand, or by suppressing an impulse to pocket a napkin holder from off the dining room table. Vershinin is also a voracious reader. In Act II, might he not absentmindedly open a book lying about and finger the pages as he brings up the rumor that his brigade may be sent elsewhere?

A look at Vershinin's first entrance in Act I to introduce himself to the three sisters will illustrate how the exercise to create ingrained character habit applies to less habitual behavior as well.

The actor playing Vershinin asks himself the two most important questions prior to making any entrance, particularly the first: "What do I bring on?" and "What's new or different upon arrival?"

This is Vershinin's first time here. There must be something different, unique about the Prozorov house. The actor's concern is to be sure the newness of Vershinin's response stays in character, that it's nuanced, to one degree or another, by habits created from all the other entrances he's made in his forty-three years. The actor might discover, through the exercise, that Vershinin is ruled by a timidity, a shrinking feeling he'd felt as a young recruit upon being summoned to his commandant's quarters. This might lead to a choice of an almost imperceptible gesture of pulling himself up to his full military bearing from an unconscious shrinking just after he crosses the threshold.

The actors playing Gertrude and Vershinin have demonstrated how craft and inspiration work together to create physical character. The next exercises will examine how craft and inspiration combine to create vocal characterization.

8.
Sound and Speech

Context

As well as offering a playgoer the pleasures of entertainment and illumination, acting is a social act during which one bears witness to life. When the sound of the actor's voice is married to the sound of the character's voice, the act of speaking expresses a witness unique to both actor and character.

The upcoming exercise focuses on sound and speech as partners in the expression of character. It looks at how to create the unique tone of the actor and character speaking as one voice. It examines the interplay between sounds and words, the working relationship between breathing and thought process, and how vowels and consonants create variations of tone. In short, the exercise provides an architecture of sound and speech for how to talk in character.

The exercise presumes the actor's voice is in good working order and does not focus on the basic mechanics of speaking. But, since it's always a good idea to refresh the basics in any discipline, here's a quick review of how we make words.

The body from which words are made is governed by the diaphragmatic muscle, which controls the breathing that determines pitch by vibrating the vocal folds, which resonates through the resonating cavities in the skull and torso to create a tone.

Human speech is comprised of three elements: (1) sound—the making of tone, (2) enunciation—the saying of vowels and consonants, and (3) articulation—the precise, combined use of tone, vowels, and consonants in the saying of words. When words are put together from a thought process to express a feeling, they form a *diction*, a manner of speaking.

A character's diction is distinguished by the character's social, cultural, psychological, psychic, and genetic influences, from which the character acquires vocabulary, pronunciation, phraseology, rhythm and tempo of speaking, use of idiomatic expressions, use of technical or professional terms, psychological mannerisms of speech, and so forth.

To give a simple illustration: Tom Wingfield has heard his mother sing out the phrase "Rise and shine! Rise and shine!" all his life. This idiomatic expression from the American South of his mother's youth is likely to make his own somewhat faded Southern accent come slightly more forward every time he uses the expression. Add to this how the psychological impact of mother on son, the irony of the cultural admonition to get up and go to work during the Great Depression, and the dimness of their dingy back-alley apartment all combine to load the simple figure of speech with character. Does Tom, for example, extend the vowels in "rise and shine" as mockery of his mother, or does he elongate the *shh* in "shine" in an unconscious attempt to keep her quiet?

Deep listening

Actor, playwright, poet, and musician all owe their success in no small measure to a heightened sense of what the musician and composer Pauline Oliveros called "deep listening."

Billie Whitelaw, performer extraordinaire of Beckett's plays, would listen to Beckett read aloud so she could absorb his resonances into her own. Many playwrights will read aloud their entire play at the first meeting of the company. They do this in the hope the actors will deep listen for the unsayable, unheard resonances in the words of the play.

Deep listening is perhaps what the novelist Ralph Ellison was alluding to when he wrote: "Who knows but that, on the lower frequencies, I speak for you?"

In rehearsals, it's not at all unusual for an actor to suggest changing lines to make them "easier to say" or "sound better." Nor is it unusual for a playwright to recognize the need for a line change, or to add a line, from the sound of an actor's voice.

Most theatre historians believe that, as an actor himself, Shakespeare had a special ability as playwright to create dialogue, as well as use dialogue created by his fellow actors. Foremost among that cooperative ensemble of actors was Richard Burbage, who was the first to play Hamlet.

In the year 1601, when Burbage spoke the "to be or not to be" soliloquy, many in the audience were uneducated and could not grasp the literal meaning of some of the words. Nevertheless, it can be argued they were able to comprehend the conundrum of mortality posed by the soliloquy because its full sense was transmitted by the vibrations of a collective intelligence in the sound of the actor's voice.

Presume an actor's body as molecular matter is yet one more transmitter of sound waves. Then might not the sound of an actor's voice, in some immeasurable way, speak from, and add to, an ever-evolving collective intelligence? It may be other than fantasy to imagine the sound waves of Burbage's voice gaining additional resonances as they pass through the bodies of the crowd and resound through the unseen matter of time and space, where they are feelingly heard by succeeding generations of actors, who deep listen to the sound of the collective intelligence.

The passion of suffering as primary sound

Speaking puts passion to use by way of language as expression of thought process. A sinner seeks absolution by spoken confession. For some, to avow love aloud is the greater gift of the feeling itself. A baby cries, a mother coos babytalk. There is a breath of passion in everything said. Each passionate response vibrates as unheard sound in the body, from which a thought process finds words to express feeling behavior as a speech act in sound with the tonal variations that suit the moment.

Each person produces a sound of their own from the tuning fork of their own body—a sound first tuned, in all likelihood, by the mother's heartbeat resonating through the water of the womb and vibrating in the unborn child. As each body matures into adulthood, it becomes a sounding instrument unique to itself.

All feeling conditions contain the unheard sound of the character's fundamental life passion of suffering. This is what I refer to as the primary sound.

And since that passion is the result of the merged passions of actor and character, as shown in the earlier exercises, the actor's own primary sound is *de facto* present as part of the character's sound. In this dynamic, the tonal vibrations of actor and character speak as one voice.

Preparation for the exercise
The Scene

Chekov never states when, if ever, Masha and Vershinin have consummated their affair. But both actor and director have assumed Chekov has made the consummation abundantly clear when he sends Masha and Vershinin off together at the end of Act II. Since it's more than a year after their first meeting, one could make an interpretive case that the affair had been consummated earlier. But the actor playing the childless Masha chooses Vershinin's declaration of love in Act II as the first time—a choice that suggests Masha, unlike her despised sister-in-law, has been struggling in vain to keep her scruples and resist her desires.

Her hapless schoolteacher husband, willfully choosing to ignore the fact of his wife's affair, continues to suffocate her with mindless devotion. Her sisters are losing control of the family house to their acquisitive sister-in-law, who's cuckolding their brother. The dream of returning to a happier life in Moscow is over. It's very late, everyone's exhausted from running ragged in response to a major fire in town. No one knows the why of all this suffering.

As she prepares to play Masha's confession scene in Act III of *Three Sisters*, the actor reminds herself that the time it takes for a sound to create words by means of a thought process is too quick to measure and that the sounds being sought are below normal hearing range. But the imagined sounds of the exercise will adjust intuitively in the playing as Masha speaks from her primary sound with all its tonal variations.

She knows from experience the exercise is long and difficult and deserves a note of caution: subtextual sounds can cause psychic disturbance because they might render the actor psychologically defenseless to an onslaught of feelings.

She reminds herself to imagine the primary sound as gathering the past, present, and future thoughts and feelings of both actor and character together in one breath—a breath meant to harness the energy of all those feelings into the spoken word. Many of these feelings are frightening and unwanted, many of them thrilling and desirable. The frightening and unwanted ones cause forcefields of psychic tension. If this happens, she knows it's best to treat the psychic muscles the same as body muscles and ease off to prevent stretching them too far before going back to exercise.

Reminder made, the actor gets ready to go to work.

The actor playing Masha has adapted the confession into a monologue and broken it into beats as preparation for the exercise.

Each changing beat will affect a change in the undertones and overtones in the sound of the previous beat, creating a different tone for the succeeding beat, and so on. Each beat, then, is a variation of a character's primary sound. Every beat is thus an integral part of an overall composition of tonal changes that make up what might be called the character's music.

Here's the breakdown following those guidelines. (The beats where tonal variation from one beat leads to the next are in bold.)

Masha: (**beat**) I want to make a confession, dear sisters. Yes, my soul is aching. I'll confess to you and never again to anyone...I'll tell you this minute (*softly*). It's my secret but you must know everything...(**beat**) I can't be silent.... I love, I love...I love that man...You just now saw him...Why don't I say it...Yes, I'll say it...I love Vershinin. (*Olga doesn't want to hear any more and takes herself out of sight, leaving Masha with Irina.* **beat**) But what can I do? (*takes her head in her hands*) At first, he seemed odd to me, then I was sorry for him...then I fell in love with him...fell in love with his voice, his words, his misfortunes, his two daughters. But what am I to do? (**beat**) I love him...It is my fate...It's my lot...And he loves me...It's all so terrible, so awful...(**beat**) But can it be so wrong? (*Masha takes Irina by the hand and draws her to herself.*) Oh, my dear...How are we going to live our lives, what is to become of us? When you read a novel it all seems so old and simple, but when you fall in love yourself, then you learn that nobody knows anything, and everyone must decide for themselves...(**beat**) My dear ones, my sisters...I have made my confession to you, and now I'll be silent...(**beat**) Like Gogol's lunatic, I'll be silent...silence....

I'll use the first two beats of the monologue to illustrate how the sound of one beat leads to the sound of another.

Masha: (**beat**) I want to make a confession, dear sisters. Yes, my soul is aching. I'll confess to you and never again to anyone...I'll tell you this minute (*softly*). It's my secret but you must know everything...(**beat**) I can't be silent.... I love, I love...I love that man...You just now saw him...Why don't I say it...Yes, I'll say it...I love Vershinin.

Notice how Chekov has captured the whole story of Masha's life in those first two beats: "my soul is aching" is a present-time characterization of her passion of suffering and "I love Vershinin" is Masha's present-time expression of her passion to survive. The actor has already exercised both life passions so that, now, they are an instinctive part of Masha's behavior in the present time of the play. The actor's ability to embody the two passions of suffering and survival are now a significant tool for using the sound exercise to release all the resonances of Masha's life ambitions into the present time of the play.

An Exercise for Speaking in Character

Part One: Incorporating the Primary Sound

Masha has just made a bitter remark about Natasha, the voracious sister-in-law. Her sister Olga berates her, calls her silly, but then asks her forgiveness.

1. Find the present passion of suffering in the scene.
The first beat of the confession occurs after a pause. Imagine the suffering Masha draws in during the breath of that pause! A dream of a better life evaporated, a dead and adored father receding from memory, her two beloved sisters chronically unhappy, a despised sister-in-law running the family in place of a disgraced brother, her secret lover tormented by a mentally disturbed wife, a dull but devilishly needy husband leaving to go to their home without her after professing his love—a love she has never returned.

2. Find the phrase.
She finds a phrase in the beat that's the interpretive heart of the primary sound. She chooses "My soul is aching." The language in the first beat (particularly the references to her sins in the plural and the yearning) makes it a good choice to reflect the passion of Masha's eternal sorrow.

3. Breathe in the passion of suffering.

She breathes in Masha's passion from the mandala of a lone oak tree by the seashore. The actor is using an image that she experienced at the opening of the play when Masha is reading Pushkin's *Ruslan and Ludmilla* on the anniversary of her father's death.

Note: Most often, it's not necessary to repeat the Exercise to Embody the Passion of Suffering. A well-trained actor will have it at the ready from doing the earlier work and need not exercise to recapture it.

Part Two: Connecting Sound to the Beat

1. Repeat the phrase.

The actor playing Masha repeats the phrase *my soul is aching* over and over silently in her mind, an unspoken mantra, until the feeling condition of the scene absorbs the passionate feeling of loss inherent in the image of the lone oak. The unheard primary sound is now present in the passionate yearning Masha feels in the scene. The sound of that passion is now the primary sound of the confession.

2. Listen for the sound of the inner life.

The actor listens for the sound of Masha's inner life. She's listening to the vibrations in her body. She's deep listening to *feel the sound* even though she may not, at first, hear it by ear.

The sound will probably occur first as a cacophony of sounds and noises. (The cacophony doesn't happen so often when an actor is well-rehearsed in the exercise.) The mix of noise and sound occurs because the exercise releases a tremendous number of mental and emotional associations, all of which are in conflict to find outlets for expression.

The actor is listening for a pure tone, not a noise—a tone that is the foundation of the exercise. A tone that will absorb the wayward activity inherent in the noise. A tone that hints of the unheard primary sound.

The tone (or a version of it) can often be heard in a key vowel of the phrase. The actor playing Masha hears the tone in the *oh* sound of *soul*.

3. Become the sound.

Now the actor makes the sound until she becomes the sound. She relaxes her body, breathes into the sound she hears, vocalizes it easily, and sustains it through one long breath. She repeats making the sound until her whole body is vibrating the sound, until she feels she's releasing the sound not just with her vocal apparatus but through every pore of her physical being. The actor has, in effect, transformed herself into the abstract, primary sound of the character's passion in present time—like a great opera singer can sometimes seem, for a moment, to disappear when holding a sustained note, leaving us to imagine that we *see* sound.

4. Connect the phrase to primary sound.

Next, the actor once more reconnects the phrase *my soul is aching* to its primary sound of Masha's passion of suffering. She continues to make the sound and think the words of the key phrase until she marries thought process to the primary sound.

5. Speak from the sound.

As she thinks the phrase *my soul is aching*, the actor again deep listens to the vibrations of the primary sound in her body. This time, rather than voice the sound aloud, she speaks the entire confession from the sound. The actor is practicing how the primary sound affects the saying of the confession.

It's most important that the actor speak *from* the sound, not try to put the sound into the words. The words are not meant to prove the sound: they are an improvised extension of the deeper sound. She continues *saying the words from the primary sound* until she can feel the certainty of how it affects every spoken word of the confession.

The primary sound is now the basis (the signature chord) from which to sound the character's tonal variations that compose what might be called the song of Masha's confession. Here, again, is the second beat of the confession as an example:

> Masha: (**beat**). I can't be silent...I love, I love...I love that man...You just now saw him...Why don't I say it...Yes, I'll say it...I love Vershinin.

Part Three: Create a Sound for the Next Beat

1. Find the key phrase.

The actor playing Masha uses *I love that man* as the key phrase for the feeling condition of the second beat.

2. Embody the feeling of the key phrase.

She uses a moment she recalls from earlier in rehearsal when her entire body filled with a joy of innocent girlhood love as Vershinin kissed her hand.

3. Locate the sound in the inner life.

The actor deep listens to *feel the sound* as it vibrates in her body. The sound is the ultimate expression of Masha's need for Vershinin's love as an act of survival.

4. Become the sound.

She makes the sound until she becomes the sound.

5. Connect the phrase to its sound.

She then makes the sound and thinks the words of the key phrase until she marries thought process to feeling condition

6. Speak from the sound.

The actor playing Masha thinks *I love that man,* deep listens to the sound as it vibrates in her body. Then, she speaks the entire second beat from the sound.

7. Repeat.

The actor repeats saying the beat from the sound until the connection is second nature.

Part Four: Create a Composition of Sounds

1. Use the key phrase.

Now that the actor playing Masha has the sounds for the first two beats of the confession to her sisters, she wants to think the key phrase *(my soul is aching)*, then say the entire first beat, then think the next key phrase (*I love that man*) and say the entire second beat.

2. Repeat to internalize the sound.

She repeats the process until she can say the two beats in sequence and no longer has to literally think the key phrases. By this time, the exercise will have achieved its purpose—for the *sound* of each beat to spontaneously adjust to the sound of the next beat and vibrate *in the actor's body* with a feeling certainty below conscious hearing.

3. Break the entire confession into sound beats.

Next, the actor breaks the entire scene of confession into beats. Here's the scene in paragraph form, with each of its five beats noted in caps, the key phrase for each beat in bold, stage directions in italics.

> Masha: (BEAT) I want to make a confession, dear sisters. Yes, **my soul is aching.** I'll confess to you and never again to anyone...I'll tell you this minute (*softly*). It's my secret but you must know everything...
>
> (BEAT) I can't be silent.... I love, I love...I love that man...You just now saw him...Why don't I say it...Yes, I'll say it...**I love Vershinin.**
>
> (*Olga doesn't want to hear any more and takes herself out of sight, leaving Masha with Irina.*)
>
> (BEAT) But what can I do? (*takes her head in her hands*) At first, he seemed odd to me, then I was sorry for him...then I fell in love with him...fell in love with his voice, his words, his misfortunes, his two daughters. But what am I to do? (BEAT) I love him...**It is my fate**...It's my lot...And he loves

me…It's all so terrible, so awful…(BEAT) But can it be so wrong? (*Masha takes Irina by the hand and draws her to herself.*) Oh, my dear…How are we going to live our lives, **what is to become of us?** When you read a novel it all seems so old and simple, but when you fall in love yourself, then you learn that nobody knows anything, and everyone must decide for themselves…

(BEAT) My dear ones, my sisters…I have made my confession to you, and now I'll be silent…(BEAT) Like Gogol's madman, I'll be silent… **silence**….

4. Continue for the rest of the beats.

The actor exercises the key phrase for each of the three remaining beats until she has a key phrase and a sound for all five beats. Then she'll be ready to practice the intrinsic musicality of the speech.

5. Create a composition of sound.

The actor playing Masha expresses the entire speech as the series of sounds. She intones the sound of all five beats in succession (no thoughts, no words) as if they were the speech as song. This, too, she repeats until it becomes a feeling certainty in her body.

6. Say the entire speech.

Finally, the actor places herself in the context of the play, motivated by the circumstance in the scene. She thinks the thought of the first beat *(my soul is aching)* and acts the speech in context, without any conscious attempt at recreating any of the work she has done in the exercises.

By the end of the exercise the actor will speak effortlessly with a spontaneous variety of tonal colors befitting Masha's character.

The battle for emphasis

Recall that every beat has a quality of tone made distinctive by the encounter between actor, character, and circumstance.

Therefore, the undertones and overtones give each beat subtextual resonances that voice a unique tonality.

In the silence that precedes her confession speech, Masha is host to an array of subtextual thoughts and feelings. Her heart and mind are filled to overflowing with things to say and do: she longs to embrace Vershinin; she's absolutely convinced her sister-in-law Natasha, who's just passed through, has purposefully burnt the coffee which smolders in her stomach; she has a vision of herself sitting on her father's lap as a child; she worries her sister Olga will have a nervous breakdown; she hears a snippet of music from *Eugene Onegin*; thinks her sister Irina's suitor, Tuzenbach, is a bore; the lamps are too low—*why doesn't someone raise the wicks?*—she wonders how old she looks to others, Vershinin's wife for instance.

And so on, and on…

Imagine the battle going on in Masha between text and subtext: each of these felt experiences—and countless more like them—are like little people, each with a need of its own fighting for attention, clambering about Masha's heart and mind, trying to find their way into her consciousness. The winner of the battle gets *emphasis.*

Four things can happen to Masha relative to the battle for emphasis:

(1) The subtext will stay subtext and the thoughts of a beat will be consistent with its interpreted action (to confess that her soul yearns for Vershinin).

(2) A conscious thought from the subtext will create a different intention, inappropriate for the intention of the moment, and the beat won't sound like what it's talking about.

(3) Conversely, the inappropriate thought could prove valuable to the actor's interpretation.

(4) If the overcrowded heart and mind of the actor playing Masha are unable to make any choices at all, she will suffer an oscillating confusion, a fumbling, stumbling, hesitant inner life that leads to forced rather than spontaneous choices.

Here are four possible results for each scenario:

(1) When the actor playing Masha interprets the desire to confess as the appropriate intention and thinks and speaks from *I love that man,* the undertones and overtones of all those little creatures of association, discovered in the homework, will make their contributions with a variety of tonal inflections, and the beat will sound like what it says.

(2) But suppose Masha's acidic stomach wins the battle for emphasis, and Masha's anger at Natasha, the maker of burnt coffee, causes her to think *oh, how I hate that despicable woman!* This in turn makes her want to take revenge—an intention inappropriate to the actor's interpretation. Masha's fury at Natasha has become more important to her than her need to confess her love for Vershinin. The tone of Masha's anger at Natasha won't sound like what it's talking about because it belies the chosen intention in the words of the beat.

(3) Imagine instead that the subtextual feeling makes the actor realize she has not put enough interpretive emphasis on Masha's irascibility, and that her love for Vershinin might not be well-earned if it's too sentimental. And suppose, for that purpose, she thinks *oh, how I hate that despicable woman!* and allows the anger at Natasha to diminish the expression of Masha's love for Vershinin. Thus, the inappropriate thought results in a differently nuanced interpretation of the moment.

(4) A forced choice can, and should, advise the actor to the need for other possibilities to find the spontaneous choice.

These are but a few examples of many possibilities that illustrate how subtextual tonalities contribute to the nuances of a complex characterization.

Other uses

The two primary sounds in a key beat are of value in preparation for performance and auditions because they exercise the sound of extreme feelings.

They also open the actor's ears to "deep listen" for the full resonance of a fellow actor's response—the secret to a consistently spontaneous performance.

Likewise, intoning all the sounds as one song of character will ensure a variety of tonalities in performance.

The exercise can also come in handy during rehearsal when the sound of a beat feels a little "off"—usually a sign the actor has not listened well enough to their fellow actor. If the actor playing Masha breathes in the vowel sound of "love" in the key phrase *I love that man,* it's likely she will reawaken the undertones and overtones that bring full resonance to the response when she goes back to the moment.

The sound exercise can also be a tool to release tension or explore a range of feeling and open oneself to further discovery in rehearsal.

The next exercise to enhance vocal characterization looks at how to breathe in character: how breathing orchestrates rhythm, tempo, and subtextual tonalities to affect interpretation of character.

9.
Breathing in Character

Context

When an actor is fully in character, both actor and character are breathing and thinking on parallel tracks at the same time. Jean Louis-Barrault, the great French actor, offered an understanding of breathing that made good account of how this happens.

The double breath

Barrault suggested the actor has a double breath: one breath for the actor and a second breath for the character. Since some portion of the breath is always active as blood oxygen, the first breath serves as the sustaining breath of the actor, over which the actor's self takes a second breath in character. In short, the actor is breathing for two.

For Barrault, this explained why the actor is always present, even while completely immersed in the character. As anecdotal backup for Barrault's understanding, one has only to recall how often an actor stands in the wings and takes a deep breath just before going on, and how, after an exit, the actor exhales a breath as if to release the life of the play. Quite often, the next breath the actor takes off stage gives life to thoughts of how the scene went that have been stored on the back burner of the mind during the playing of it. (Recall the experience of the actor playing Tom in in Chapter 6, Inspiration.)

The actor's first breath is involuntary. The actor's second breath, when taken in character, becomes the character's involuntary first breath. A character may breathe only if the actor supplies him with his first involuntary breath to do so. This activity is the basis for breathing in character.

What thought a character has, and where they breathe it in, is a guarantee of spontaneity.

Patterns of breathing

Rhythm is a pattern of stressed beats, and tempo is the rate of speed at which the pattern occurs. Rhythm and tempo, though defined separately, are so inextricably bound to each other as to be thought of as inseparable. The tempo of breathing combined with the rhythmic emotional stresses of thought processes and their feelings make up a character's diction, its way of speaking, its style, what we might call the arrangement of the character's song.

Alterations of rhythm and tempo are a significant way to express an interpretive character choice. For example, Laurence Olivier suggested the right way to do Shakespeare is to breathe in the wrong place—once. Numbers being arbitrary, here's a breathing pattern of a beat in Hamlet's "O what a rogue" soliloquy that pays due attention to the five-beat iambic line.

> "O what a rogue and peasant slave am I! (breath)
> Is it not monstrous that this player here, (breath)
> But in a fiction, in a dream of passion, (breath)
> Could force his soul so to his own conceit ....

Now, an example of the "wrong" place, as Olivier suggested, with an added breath for emphasis as an aspect of character (the added breath in bold). Note how breathing changes word stress with ease to effect interpretation.

> "O what a rogue and peasant slave am I! (breath)
> Is it not monstrous that this player here,
> But in a fiction, **(breath)** in a dream of passion,
> (breath) Could force his soul so to his own conceit ....

After establishing the rhythm and tempo of the verse in the first two lines, the actor moves the breath at the end of the second line to within the third line to interrupt the flow of the verse. The stop-and-go rhythm caused by the added breath suggests that Hamlet is already unconsciously working his way from self-reproach to intended action by the end of the scene. This is a slight change in the breathing of the lines that is valuable to the actor's interpretation: to arrive at a nearly manic glee when Hamlet realizes that Claudius's reaction to the "fiction" of the play will prove he murdered Hamlet's father and free Hamlet to take revenge.

The more overt musicality of verse dialogue lends itself easily to vocal arranging. A look at a speech of Vershinin's in Act II of *Three Sisters* will illustrate how the less apparent but equally rich music of prose dialogue can be scored by an actor.

Preparation for the Exercise

Vershinin and Masha are in the darkened drawing room. They've become utterly enamored of each other in the year since they met. The lighted candles in the dining room create a shadow portrait of their love for each other. Perhaps they see only each other's eyes as they murmur their lovers' talk. Vershinin will shortly say, speak, declare, proclaim the words "I love you," to the "splendid, wonderful woman," Masha.

Vershinin is describing—as lovers are wont to do in prologue to professions of love—the unhappiness of his life, the need for the balm of her love.

> I haven't had any dinner, nothing to eat since the morning. My daughter's not well, and when my girls are ill, I get so anxious my conscience tortures me because they have such a mother. Oh, if you had seen her today! What a petty-minded woman! We began quarrelling at seven in the morning and at nine I slammed the door and went out. (*pause*) It's strange...I never speak of her...Only to you...I complain only to you. (*kisses her hand*) Don't be angry with me...I have no one but you...no one....

The first thing the actor playing Vershinin wants to establish is the character's habitual pattern of speaking. In addition to the contributions made by the character's emotional behavior to the way Vershinin talks, the actor wants to add the social and cultural influences on Vershinin as a major influence on the character's habitual pattern of speech.

At the end of the nineteenth century, Vershinin's manner of speech would be greatly affected by the historical conflict in the Russian soul between its "barbaric" Asiatic roots and its "civilized" ambition to be European. These influences contribute to Vershinin's habitual manner of speaking. The class ambition of a young Russian bourgeoisie was to be well spoken, and certainly Vershinin, in his brave and foolish attempt to live a rational, enlightened life in a suffering Russia, would be prone to the phrasings and cadences inherent in the rhythm of such a cultural influence. By the time Vershinin has reached maturity, these influences would have become so habitual a pattern of breathing they would go largely unnoticed.

The actor playing Vershinin will use the first part of the upcoming exercise to establish a habitual pattern of breathing as a grid from which he will establish how the character's emotional behavior creates the rhythm and tempo of Vershinin's speech in the present time of the play. As we saw with the actor playing Masha in the Exercise for Speaking in Character, the actor playing Vershinin will have already exercised the character's variety of tonal colors from Vershinin's primary sound.

An Exercise for Breathing in Character

1. Breathe in the character's habitual pattern.

The actor starts with Vershinin's habitual pattern of speech as a man who prides himself on his ability to deal with his feelings in an educated, rational way. The breaths are in parentheses.

> (breath) I haven't had any dinner, nothing to eat since this morning. (breath) My daughter's not well, (breath) and when my girls are ill, I get so anxious my conscience tortures me because they have such a mother. (breath) Oh, if you had seen her today! (breath) What a petty-minded woman! (breath) We began quarrelling at seven in the morning and at nine I slammed the door and went out. (breath) It's strange... (breath) I never speak about her... (breath) Only to you...I complain only to you. (breath—kisses her hand—breath). Don't be angry with me... (breath) I have no one but you...no one....

2. Repeat until habitual.
3. Add the breaths from the present-time feeling in the play.

The actor interprets Vershinin to be carrying a conflicted guilt and torment for marrying badly, and in the pressure of the moment, his attempt to declare his love for Masha is not quite rational. To reveal yet more of Vershinin's character, the actor adds three noticeable breaths (in bold) where the intensity of feeling interrupts the character's habit of rational discourse.

> (breath) I haven't had any dinner, nothing to eat since this morning. (breath) My daughters are not well, (breath) and when my girls are ill, I get so anxious **(breath)** my conscience tortures me because they have such a mother. (breath) Oh, if you had seen her today! (breath) What a petty-minded woman! (breath) We began quarrelling at seven in the morning and at nine **(breath)** I slammed the door and went out. (breath) It's strange... (breath) I never speak about her... (breath) Only to you...I complain only to you.

(breath—he takes her hand—**breath**—kisses her hand—breath). Don't be angry with me... (breath) I have no one but you... (breath) no one....

After "My daughters are not well," the actor holds Vershinin's habitual breath just a bit longer to give a subtle, added emphasis to the fractured feelings he endures in his marriage.

The added breath after "I get so anxious" and before "my conscience tortures me" disturbs Vershinin's habitual attempt to compose himself in a civilized manner as it starts to release the intensity of Vershinin's torment in the scene. This motivates further his increasing need for Masha's love in the rest of the play.

The added breath before he speaks of slamming the door on his wife suggests a darker side to Vershinin's anger.

The added breath after he takes Masha's hand suggests he orders himself to give in to his feeling for Masha; it takes him out of the material world into the utopian elsewhere inspired by this "splendid woman."

Altogether, the added breaths contribute an intensity of feeling that betrays Vershinin's cultural notion of himself as a rational, civilized person.

It's worth a reminder that nuanced interpretive choices are spontaneous when the actor has created subtext from the character's past experiences. For example: Vershinin's intake of breath before "I slammed the door" might include the sense memory of an earlier time when he banged his fist on the door to avoid striking his wife. He might experience it as a sting in his right hand that colors how he speaks to Masha. All this feeling inspires a breath taken in "the wrong" place that adds a tension of unpredictability to the moment and gives added suspense to the entire scene.

As an aside, the inherent pathology of holding one's breath can be useful in characterization. For examples, a physically or mentally disordered person often has difficulty breathing out, as if the sickness itself needed the toxicity of the carbon dioxide; a child will sometime defend itself from a scolding or refuse unwanted food by holding its breath—a willfulness which inevitably leads to tantrum and tears.

Having added a pattern of breathing to the act of speaking as part of the work on gesture and movement, the actor has fully integrated the character's physical behavior. It's time now to look at how place affects characterization.

10.
Place

Context

Playwrights choose place with great care. Richard II incarcerated at Pontefract Castle behaves much differently than when he holds court at Windsor. Blanche Dubois, rather than accept that a streetcar named Desire has left her on a curtained-off cot next to the kitchen of her sister's low-rent apartment in New Orleans, fantasizes she's dancing gaily at a Cotillion Ball in Mississippi. Peter meets his death in *Zoo Story* because he's put his claim to self-esteem on a bench in Central Park.

Where a scene happens is vital to *what* happens in it. Place is as much a character in every scene as people, and its conscious and unconscious effects on a character's emotional behavior deserve the same attention to detail.

What's under consideration here is how the social, psychological, cultural, historical, and psychic resonances inherent in place contribute to character behavior.

Consciously or unconsciously, everything about place and the objects in it affects a person, and these effects can be either positive or negative. Every element of place, to one degree or another, becomes a part of the atmosphere and ambience of every play and thus of every moment of behavior in a scene.

There are three elements of place that are fundamental to understanding how it affects character behavior on stage.

(1) It is situated in a *space* designated by boundaries.

(2) It has *mass*—architectural form and the objects (set pieces and props) contained in it.

(3) Space and mass combine with lighting to create *atmosphere*.

The space of a setting might be open or closed, light or dark, and its boundaries may be defined by architectural structure or by light. Spatial boundaries help to create an aesthetic of place because they're instrumental in defining the energy of place. Its boundaries might be near or far, horizontal in line or vertical, diagonal, or circular. The open sky over the plains of Agincourt creates a different energy than that of an eight-foot ceiling in the cheap motel room in Shepard's *Fool for Love.*

The mass that occupies space can be, in its primary form, interior or exterior, or sometimes both. The form, in turn, has function. The train station in Dürrenmatt's *The Visit* brings the outside world to the poverty-stricken town. The metaphorical doll's house, in the title of Ibsen's play, a seemingly safe haven for love and marriage, functions in feeling reality as a well-appointed holding pen to keep Nora under house arrest. The objects in a setting (set pieces and props) can be natural or manmade, as in the rock on which Aeschylus's Prometheus has been bound or the wagon hauled through the Thirty Years War by Mother Courage in Brecht's play.

A *preexisting atmosphere* of place is represented by phenomenal conditions such as climate, weather, topography, time of day, and natural light. The storm on the heath in *King Lear* affects behavior differently than the suffocating humid stillness in Act I of *The Seagull.* The preexisting atmosphere becomes the *overall atmosphere* with each character's sensory responses to the forms and objects in the scene. The haze of light from an oil lamp at Macbeth's castle gate affects the drunken porter's senses differently than Lady Macbeth's. The touch of a woman's hand is different to the lustful Boniface than to the romantic Romeo. The smell of the food eaten in the Prozorov dining room affects each diner differently. The wine Masha drinks in the company of others tastes different than the wine she drinks with Vershinin. Each of the three sisters hears the troops leaving town forever with different ears.

Every story a play tells is part of the never-ending story of civilization itself, and the mass and objects which make up place are an implicit part of that story. Natural forms tend to represent the prehistoric and universal foundation of the ongoing story, while the temporal nature of manmade forms and objects tell the story itself. Prometheus's rock is a subliminal reminder for today's audience that, despite humankind's exploration of space, we are still bound to the rock of our planet. Mother Courage's wagon is a subliminal reminder of a highspeed train from Cologne to Brussels and the history of human travel.

When the lights come up for Act IV in *Three Sisters*, the audience will find themselves on the verandah of the Prozorov residence in a provincial town in turn-of-the-century Russia. If the actor playing Irina believes in the garden, the audience's belief will be confirmed. If she doesn't believe, neither will the audience. After all, the audience has volunteered their willing suspension of disbelief in order to experience the perils of unsatisfied human love on the condition that it take place in a turn-of-the-nineteenth-century provincial Russian garden on a spring morning.

An actor's failure to respond to the reality of place insults the imaginations of both the designer and audience and injures the spirit of the unwritten contract between the actual and the make-believe.

Imagine that an actor playing Irina has heard the call to places for the fourth act and is in the wings waiting to make her entrance. Her backstage reality consists of metal and lumber structures, bleached muslin, screws, nails, angle irons, lighting cable, and gaffer's tape. Among the many doodles on the back of the flat where she stands, ready to enter, is a caricature of the director drawn by a member of the company who spares no one's vanity. She suppresses a chuckle at the drawing while the prop man, sniffling from a winter cold, hands her a non-breakable prop glass with enough ginger ale to represent a last swallow of champagne to take with her into an onstage world of soft breezes and spring sunshine.

Imagine, further, how the actor, after having made a conscious effort to focus on a piece of glow tape in order to find her way to the right place in the dark, and having been mindful to get there quietly, believes she is in the Prozorov garden when the lights come up twenty-seven seconds later.

With a familiar reminder that once done is not enough and that attention to detail, breathing, and repetition are the keys to success, the next exercise will show us how she gets there ready for lights up and ready to play Irina's critical scene with Tuzenbach believing she is in the garden of the Prozorov household.

Preparation for the exercise

Irina admits only to fondness and affection for Baron Tuzenbach and is unable or unwilling to open her heart to accept his obsessive love. They are nevertheless to be married tomorrow. Yesterday, Tuzenbach argued with Solyony over Irina, and now he's on his way to engage Solyony in a duel. Does Irina know Tuzenbach is going off to fight a duel with Solyony? Chekov offers the actor no overt clue because Irina says nothing of it. Later, she merely acquiesces when Tuzenbach refuses to let her go with him. But since Irina has heard rumors—and has earlier been cornered by the stalking passion of Solyony's obsession for her—the actor makes a fair assumption that Irina knows about the duel on a subliminal level, a repressed knowledge that manifests itself as a terrible foreboding.

The actor interprets Irina's foreboding as composed of everything happening in Irina's life on this very day in the Prozorov garden: the troops moving to another barracks, leaving the already unhappy family friendless in this provincial town; the tension hovering in the air around Tuzenbach; the necessity of having to marry to a man for whom she has no romantic love. But Tuzenbach is her only escape from her dreary life. From this whirl of misery, she impulsively asks him what happened yesterday, but instead of telling her about the argument and the impending duel, he talks of loving her even as he knows she doesn't love him. As Tuzenbach starts to take his leave, Irina announces she's going with him, but he quickly refuses to let her join him. Then, just before his exit, Tuzenbach turns back to Irina. To say what? That she can go with him? To tell her what happened yesterday? But Tuzenbach says only, 'I didn't have any coffee this morning. Tell them to make me some," and leaves Irina frightened and alone.

An Exercise of Place

1. Specify the elements of the scene.

The open space of the Prozorov garden is in the bright light of noon. An avenue of fir trees leads to a river and the woods beyond. There's a table on the verandah with empty bottles and glasses; some farewell drinks having been shared. In the background, brother Andrey rocks a pram. There are sounds of troops getting ready to leave town, two years after their arrival at the start of the play. There's a light breeze stirring the air, a cloud passes over the sun. People are bustling as they come and go. The fecund soil smells of spring. Earth, sky, river, house, and woods form the boundaries of the place where the scene happens—a scene which proves to be the last time Irina and Baron Tuzenbach will see each other.

2. Find past experiences of place.

The actor playing Irina sets out to create a detailed history of experience for everything in the scene and to use sense memory to commit those experiences to Irina's memory bank.

She finds as many sensory responses to her surroundings as it takes to inspire the reality of everything in the place. The abstractly painted backdrop of trees and river will become real when the fresh smell of firs recall Irina getting lost the first week they arrived from Moscow. A roll of manufactured garden grass will become real when it provides a cushion for her feet like it was the snow of her childhood. The table on the verandah will become real when Irina remembers Olga bought it in Moscow years ago from a scrunched-up old man in St. Peter's Square. An empty champagne glass will remind Irina she's losing the drunken Chebutykin, whom she loves like a father. The splashing of the boats being made ready will call to mind that the troops first came here two years ago—and how very much older she's become in only these two years.

3. Find the critical moment in the scene.

The actor looks for a critical moment in the scene that leads up to the climactic moment when Tuzenbach stops her from going with him. She finds it in the shudder Irina experiences just before she says, "Somehow everything frightens me today."

4. Choose an appropriate experience from the play to motivate the critical moment.

Now, the actor playing Irina looks for an experience from the play rather than one from the character's life before it.

By this time, Irina's been forced to share a room with her sister Olga because her brother Andrey's wife, Natasha, has taken over her room for their baby. Irina, even as she resented Natasha's taking over their house, had been powerless to refuse the request. The morning after she lost her room to Natasha's manipulations, Irina suffered the further humiliation of Natasha leaning over the verandah railing cooing a "good morning" to her as if nothing had happened. Since then, Irina has been having a recurring dream of being locked in a dungeon. The verandah railing becomes her connection to place for the critical moment.

5. Connect a sense memory to the object in the scene.

The actor connects the sound of Natasha's voice by holding onto the verandah railing until the connection between sound and railing become a certainty.

6. Internalize the sound and its feeling to the critical moment.

The verandah railing now available to the actor, she exercises the *sight* of the railing and the sickeningly sincere *sound* of Natasha's cooing until the feeling of claustrophobia makes her want to escape and *motivates the dread* that makes her say "everything frightens me today." The sound of Natasha's cooing, and the dread that causes the shudder connected to it, are now anchored to the reality of place by the presence of the veranda.

7. Repeat the connection until it becomes habit.

8. Play the critical moment in the context of the scene.

As she plays the scene, the dread will be available to her as an unconscious nuance throughout the scene. The actor chooses to have Irina consciously hear Natasha's cooing to motivate a shudder in the critical moment and later in the scene she Irina will see the verandah bars in her mind's eye in the climactic moment when Tuzenbach prevents her attempt to go with him.

Having exercised herself into a felt reality of place, the actor playing Irina has accomplished four things:

(1) She's made place real for herself and enhanced her ability for consistently spontaneous behavior.

(2) The felt reality of place has inspired a more resonant interpretation of the character's dilemma.

(3) By making place real for herself, she has kept her unspoken bargain with the audience: to confirm the fictional presentation of place as a felt reality.

(4) She's put her body at ease and eliminated the tension inherent in trying to live in two places at once. A body at home in its surroundings is more likely to behave with an

ease that makes the actor's playing of character choices more spontaneous.

Other uses

Two things are helpful for making place a reality performance after performance.

First, the actor can go onstage before the house opens and take the time to experience the sensory values of place; she can wander about the set, free-associating into the play, touch the table and dream of Moscow, smell the champagne and worry about Andrey's gambling, taste the air and laugh at the irony of Tuzenbach's love for her, hear the breeze and remember the fire, see the curtains in the window and spin the top that was her name-day present two years ago.

Second, she can prepare for a given performance with any of the other experiences she worked with in step 2, finding past experiences of place, as they occur to her. Suppose the actor discovered how a carelessly discarded champagne glass moved Irina to despair at her wasted life. The glass itself has also come to embody the felt actuality of place. One glance from the wings at the discarded champagne glass will bring to life the house and verandah, the woods, the trees, the river, the noonday sun. In this way, place will, unselfconsciously, become whole.

Earning the choices that make for an actor's singular interpretation of a character is the work of the next chapter.

11.
Earning Choices

Context

A play enters the collective intelligence and becomes part of a classical canon of dramatic literature when it dramatizes the passions of certain persons in a certain time as a universal metaphor for the human condition. Sophocles' tragedy *Oedipus the King*, written around 425 B.C.E, has entered the canon of Western dramatic literature.

The play abounds with contrasts that reflect an epochal, universal struggle between barbarism and civilization: Oedipus's pride and fury have a mythological barbaric quality in contrast to his brother-in-law Creon's idea of a more rational rule of Thebes. Contrasts of night and day, light and dark, reason and prophecy, knowledge and ignorance, belonging and not belonging, grandiosity and paranoia, pride and humility are aptly mirrored in the particulars of Oedipus's feelings, within social and cultural constructs of orphanhood and family, freeborn and slave, low-born and royal adoption, outlaw and citizen.

Sophocles' choice of self-blinding for the climactic action of the play satisfies as metaphor for the human condition because it abounds with these and many other resonances. When a character's choice for the climactic action becomes a metaphor for a universal life condition, it enters the collective intelligence where it is passed from generation to generation.

In the dramatic art of theatre, a choice is passed from author to character to audience. The linchpin of that process is the actor.

Choice and the critical moment

A series of scenes throughout a play contains a series of critical moments of varying degrees of intensity, building to the moment of choice for the climactic action. It's the nature of a critical moment that it contains any number of choices for the character other than the one written in the play. All choices, thus, should run the risk that a character will choose an action rather than the one written in the play. In other words, in a moment of crisis, anything is possible.

The less intense moments of pressure will, naturally, arouse fewer possible choices. However, as the character nears the climactic moment and the lesser crises increase in intensity, the number of other possible actions accumulates, and the pressure increases on the character. The result is a chaotic whirlwind of possible actions, which intensifies the risk the character might, indeed, make a different choice.

The first time

Oedipus, King of Thebes, has unknowingly fulfilled a prophecy that he would murder his father, marry his mother, and sire incestuous children. Upon hearing the truth, he goes into the palace and stabs out his eyes.

Imagine the first performance of the play when the first Oedipus makes the critical choice to blind himself before he goes offstage to commit the act. Imagine, further, the chaos of endless possibilities for action that must have been whirling in Oedipus's mind and body at the moment he hears the truth. Now, imagine the physical agony, the shame and terror, the crushing burden of his guilt, and the strange humility he feels from committing the act that seals his fate. Imagine how the power of that feeling would have radiated out from an amplifying mask to an amphitheater filled with thousands of spectators.

From the first performance of the play nearly 2500 years ago to today, that first actor and every actor playing Oedipus since have been, in their own time and their own place, challenged to play that critical moment when Oedipus looks at the sun and says, "... O Light, may I look on you nevermore!" as if it has never been said before. Then each actor is further challenged when Oedipus goes off, blinds himself, and returns with bloodied eye sockets—both choices played *for the first time, every time* by the thousands upon thousands of actors who have followed in the role, one production after another, throughout the millennia.

Perhaps this is what Stella Adler referred to when she advised actors that the measure of their talent was in the quality and daring of their choices.

Earning the choice

The next two exercises deal with how an actor playing King Oedipus can *earn* the climactic choice of blinding himself by taking that risk.

The first, An Exercise to Improvise Possible Choices, deals with the physical chaos of possible actions. The second, An Exercise to Improvise Irrational Thought Process, deals with the mental chaos of thoughts. The purpose of the first exercise is to embody in muscle memory the habit of a possibility that anything could happen at any time. The second is to store in the actor's memory bank the potential for a mental breakdown. The combined physical and mental exercises will create a subtextual habit of possible choices that will assure the actor puts their choice at risk in order to earn it.

Some actors would prefer to do the exercises alone because they are so extreme. Many actors are hesitant the first few times around, and some are downright terrified of them because, simply said, every crisis a character suffers is a step on a journey to potential madness—a demand that calls for an irrational, no-holds-barred expression of the most primitive impulses.

Preparation

The first exercise is in three parts and is predicated on establishing the worst and best reactions to a crisis as set pieces of opposite extremes. These are the extremes from which the actor improvises a chaos of possible actions.

The exercise is irrational, silent, preverbal; it is concerned with *doing* not thinking or speaking. *Do* is the operative word here. Sounds such as noises, humming, grunting, and so forth, can be made if they are a natural accompaniment to action. (Words will come later in the second exercise.)

The actions in the exercise are difficult to rehearse when working alone, but they can be played well when the actor applies his skills: the effective use of mime, employment of what's at hand for props when suitable, and the use of his senses.

The improvisation is centered on physical actions that will become the subtextual impulses from which a choice will be earned.

If the actor is working alone, it's important to know the scene well enough to work the exercise. Mime should be substituted for any physically dangerous actions. The exercise requires the actor to resist the desire to make sense or find a rationale to justify any one impulse.

Because the critical moment contains endless possibilities of actions, the assumption is the exercise might never exhaust itself unless a time limit is set. Twenty minutes or so is a good amount of time for the improvisation. A sufficiently loud alarm would make a good referee.

An Exercise to Improvise Possible Choices

Part One: Improvisation for the Best and Worst Set Pieces

1. Choose a critical moment.

An old shepherd confirms that Laius was Oedipus's father and concludes by saying: "Then may the gods pity you! For you were born to misery."

The actor playing Oedipus recognizes that the critical moment happens immediately after a stunned Oedipus accepts the horrific truth with his reply.

> Ah me! Wretched me! All brought to pass! All true!
> O light, may I look on you nevermore!
> I, Oedipus, am forever cursed. At birth, in wedlock,
> by my father's blood, my dear children shamed.

This is the specific moment when Oedipus is beset with a whirlwind of conflicted feelings calling for a chaos of possible actions—the moment from which Oedipus will choose to blind himself and proclaim his sin to the people of Thebes.

From the chaos of feelings and possible actions in that moment, the actor will improvise to find the worst and best of possible actions to use as set pieces (excluding Oedipus's action to blind himself) from which to improvise many other possible actions. In Part Two of the exercise, the actor will commit the physical expressions of the improvisations to muscle memory, where they will become a subtextual instinctive response from which anything can happen—an instinct that will earn Oedipus (and the actor) the choice to blind himself.

2. Improvise the worst and best extremes of action in the critical moment.

Consider that the moment contains, among all its possibilities, Oedipus's stubbornness, a blind fury, his transcendent love of family, an assault on his pride, a shuddering weakness, impotence, a cold fear of death, his self-loathing, a longing for human comfort, and so on. The actor playing Oedipus feels all these emotions as one dominant feeling of foreboding fear and shame.

From this feeling the actor experiences two opposing impulses: the impulse for the *worst* thing the feeling makes him want to do and the impulse for the *best* thing the feeling makes him want to do. (I suggest starting with the worst action simply because the actor will feel better by ending the exercise with the best action.)

3. Imagine the worst action.

Oedipus's feeling of foreboding fear and shame calls forth from the actor an impulse to amputate his murderous hand with a serrated knife.

4. Act out the worst action.

The actor rehearses the worst action by using the blunt edge of a serrated knife to simulate the action until he can play it truthfully and spontaneously.

5. Imagine the best action.

Once the worst action of cutting off his hand is set, the actor returns to the feeling of foreboding fear and shame and imagines the best action he could do. He recalls that in rehearsal his fellow actor's eyes were filled with fear and awe when he told Oedipus the truth. For the exercise, he imagines Oedipus saw the shepherd's fear and awe as a misery equal to his own. He then imagines the best action would be to embrace the shepherd as a brother in the awfulness of their mutual fates.

6. Act out the best action.

He rehearses the action of embracing the shepherd until it, too, can be played truthfully and spontaneously.

Once the two actions have become the beginning and end set pieces, the actor is ready for the body of the exercise in Steps 6 through 9.

An important note: The actor will not finish any action, *including the two rehearsed worst and best actions*. As described below, when he's *completely absorbed in the feeling life of each action*, the actor asks himself what he wants to do next and improvises a new action from the previous unresolved one. From the improvisation that comes out of the beginning worst scene, each new improv creates a *new feeling,* which creates a new improvisation, which creates a *new feeling,* which creates a new improv, and so on. The *only* improvisation to resolve is the action that comes out of the last improv of the best scene.

7. The improvisation for the worst action.

The actor playing Oedipus starts the *worst action* of amputating his hand. The improvised actions will be guided mostly by character, but some will be from the actor's imagination or experience, as in the following example: once the actor, in a fury as the blood flows from his arteries, asks himself what he wants to do, he answers with an impulse to blare out a trumpet version of a Sousa march—immediately, without hesitation, without pausing to wonder at the absurdity of it.

8. The next improvisation out of the first improvisation.

Once the actor is completely absorbed in the triumphant release of the march, but before he blares out the last note to bring it to an end, he asks himself what he wants to do next. Let's say he bursts into tears and starts to wipe his eyes to clear his vision. He wipes and he wipes and he wipes, he can't stop wiping.

9. Another improvisation from out of the previous.

Again, when he is completely absorbed with wiping his eyes but before he has succeeded in clearing them, he improvises his way into the next action, and the next action, and the next action, and so on. When the alarm goes off to signal the approaching end of the exercise, the actor—immediately and arbitrarily—starts to act out Oedipus's *best action*: to embrace the shepherd.

10. The last improvisation.

In the fullness of feeling his embrace of the shepherd, the actor improvises one last action. Say a dance of joy and a bow to a standing ovation. This is the only action of the entire exercise to get resolved.

11. Repeat for more possible actions.

Once the actor has completed the first round of improvisations, and after he has taken whatever break is necessary to relax from the emotional and physical demands of the exercise, he repeats the exercise as often as he can, *using the same worst and best actions* as beginning and end, mindful not to repeat any of the previous improvisations.

The actor's intention is to make himself available to as many possibilities of action in the moment as he can. He could do the exercise every day for the rest of his life and never have to repeat any one of the improvised actions. Although he may not be able to articulate the meaning of Oedipus's actions, the exercise will help him feel the prophetic certainty of it in the playing.

Next, the actor will create a montage of the improvisations, from which he will create the muscle memory to internalize them so that in Part Three he will have them available as subtextual instinct.

Part Two: Internalize the Possible Actions
as Muscle Memory

1. Create a visual montage from the improvised actions.

The actor playing Oedipus creates and relives a montage of the many unfinished improvised actions in the movie of his mind.

2. Run the montage in the critical moment.

The actor runs the montage in his mind's eye in the silence of the critical moment just before he says, "O light, may I look on you nevermore!"

3. Repeat.

He repeats the process a few times to internalize the montage as muscle memory. Because the actor has exercised the actions in his body, the montage will link muscle memory to the critical moment.

4. Work different actions from the montage to launch the beat that leads to the climactic action.

He launches the beat many times, responding each time from a prompt of a *different action* from the montage. Some examples might be the Sousa trumpet, the wiping of the eyes, digging his own grave with his bare hands, howling a rage against fate, embracing the shepherd, a happy tap dance to obliterate his misery, a frenzied search for a blade to amputate his hand, and so on.

In this way, the actor reminds himself that, from one performance to the next, spontaneity of choice in the real time of playing results from the *shifting emphases* of unconscious feelings. It also encourages him to keep alive the risk that anything could happen.

As we saw in many instances throughout most of these exercises, the art of the gesture is a most useful way to express the presence of subtextual character behavior stored in body memory.

The actor playing Oedipus next looks for an instinctive, unconscious gesture in the critical moment that will carry the subtextual presence of all the conflicted feelings, and the chaos of their possible actions, as felt reality into the critical moment.

Part Three: Translate Body Memory into Gestural Behavior

1. Find a choice of gesture.

He reviews the actions of the exercise and works with one he intuitively feels would best serve as a possible other action in the real time of the critical moment. Say, for instance, that in a fury at one point in the exercise, he had attempted to strangle the shepherd who had told him the awful truth. The actor works Oedipus's feeling of fury into the gesture of strangling the shepherd.

2. Find an instinct to stop the completion of the first action.

Obviously, if the actor playing Oedipus follows his impulse, the play will not move forward to its required end. So next, he will search to reduce the strangling of the shepherd to an unconscious, subtextual nuance by looking for an instinctive reaction that will prevent Oedipus from strangling the shepherd.

The actor has interpreted Oedipus's love of family, shown so expressly in his fatherly concerns for his daughters at the end of the play, to be equally as passionate as his pride and the fury of his ambition. He realizes Oedipus had seen the anguished face of Jocasta when she rushed into the palace in the previous scene.

The actor works the image of Jocasta's anguish in his mind's eye, over and over, until the feeling to comfort her is married to the image. Then he exercises to stop the action of strangling the shepherd by flashing the image of Jocasta's anguished face. Oedipus's fury at the shepherd is replaced with his need to comfort Jocasta. He repeats this until—in the flash of a split-second—Oedipus's instinct to reach for the shepherd's throat is stopped before his arms are extended past his elbows.

3. Reconnect the presence of the montage of other actions to the hand gesture.

The exercise needs one other small, but important, detail. The actor's intention now is to make sure the flash of Jocasta's anguish does not eliminate the ever-present risk of other possible actions inherent in the chaos of Oedipus's feelings.

At one point, for instance, as he works making the connection, the montage motivates a brief glance onto the upturned palm of his right hand, where he sees Jocasta's face—connection made.

4. Repeat to create muscle memory of the gesture.

Repeat the action until the montage is a split-second flash of muscle memory that embodies the risk of other choices for the critical moment signified by seeing Jocasta's face in his upturned palm.

5. Activate both gestures in present time.

The actor playing Oedipus works the two gestures in sequence: the reach to strangle the shepherd followed by the upturned palm with the image of Jocasta's face to abort the first gesture to strangle the shepherd. He repeats the sequence as many times as necessary to ensure both gestures are committed to the same risk of other possible choices. The result is an instinctive, spontaneous double gesture that happens so quickly it seems like a single gesture. A gesture that adds immeasurably to the subliminal suspense of the moment without corrupting the more important spoken gesture, "O light, may I look on you nevermore!" which makes the climactic action inevitable.

Oedipus's love of family, his desire for innocence, his kingship, his pride, his rage, his shame and guilt, and more, are all present in a gesture fraught with risk because it carries the unconscious chaos of other possible actions that make the gesture truly spontaneous.

We've seen throughout earlier exercises how thinking in character is necessary to spontaneous behavior. So, too, the conflicting extremes of Oedipus's thought processes are needed to further ensure the spontaneous behavior (the gesture of the upturned palm) discovered in the Exercise to Improvise Possible Choices.

Earlier we saw how a potentially deadly physical illness helped the actor playing Gertrude determine the character's physical behavior. In the following exercise, the actor playing Oedipus will show how a potential mental disorder can help characterize the thought process that motivates physical behavior.

When the two exercises work together, they carry into every critical moment, of whatever intensity, the subtextual possibilities of a different choice in both thought and deed.

An Exercise to Improvise Irrational Thought Process

1. Choose an analogous mental disorder.
The actor playing Oedipus notes that, in Scene I, when Oedipus accuses Creon and Teiresias, the blind seer, of plotting against him, he displays symptoms of a potential mental breakdown: a quickness of temper, an excessive pride, suspicion, paranoia. This behavior and the actor's experience from the exercise of the best and worst actions make a fair case that Oedipus's mental state is precarious.

The actor makes an analogy that Oedipus's mental condition is what's known to many contemporary analysts as bipolar disorder. He presumes that Oedipus would have to be in a manic state to go through the flurry of actions he takes in the play.

2. Research the symptoms.
The actor researches the symptoms of a manic episode. His research leads him to these symptoms: euphoria, enormous energy, irritability, lack of sleep, lack of judgment, inability to think clearly.

3. Change venue of the beat.
The actor performs the beat as if he is talking to a psychiatrist in a mental health facility. Further, he plays it as if he were without medication while in the grip of clinical mania. His objective is to prove to the doctor he is sane, even while his irrational thought process rules his feelings.

4. Play the beat.
In the example below, the actor says aloud both the dialogue in the critical beat and what he's thinking until he talks himself into the next moment of dialogue. He will say a line from the play in his manic state and improvise more

dialogue from that manic state until something he says makes him afraid he's not making sense to the doctor, and then he says the next line of dialogue trying to prove he's all right. He keeps this up, play dialogue followed by improvised dialogue, followed by play dialogue, followed by improvised dialogue, and so on.

As with the physical behavior in the Exercise to Improvise Possible Choices, the improvised dialogue here should be irrational, uncontrolled by logic, and will likely include the personal thoughts of the actor/character, if and when they occur.

All dialogue, written and improvised, should function as an attempt to prove Oedipus is a rational, sane person.

Here's a version of the beat with a condensed version of the improvised dialogue in bold italics. (In full practice, the improvised dialogue would be more extended to produce more irrational highs and lows.)

In response to the shepherd's revelation, a stunned Oedipus reacts by saying, "Ah me! Wretched me! All brought to pass! All true!" Then the moment for a critical choice from all possibilities happens.

Oedipus:
why are you looking at me like that?...
...where am I?...
O light, may I look on you nevermore!
...he was trembling...HELP!...
I, Oedipus...
No, really, I'm okay...I said, I'm okay!
am forever cursed. At birth,
...am I bleeding? ...where did that bicycle come from?...
in wedlock,
...spiders are crawling in my throat...no, really...I think...the weather...I mean...
by my father's blood,
I used to have a favorite color, but...

my children shamed
...the blood...STOP!...

5. Repeat.

The actor exercises the beat as many times with as many different uncensored, no-holds-barred ad libs as needed to establish with certainty his connection to the chaos of the actor/character's thought process. Once done, he's ready to bring the results to the real time of the scene.

6. Find the phrase.

He looks for a phrase from the improvisation to use in the preparation of the scene: a thought closely aligned to what Oedipus might be thinking. Often it can be found as cousin to the gesture discovered in the previous exercise—in this case, aborting the reach to strangle the shepherd by seeing Jocasta's face in his upturned palm. In our condensed example the phrase could be *...the blood...STOP!...*

7. Link thought process to the montage.

The actor exercises the key phrase *...the blood...STOP!...* over and over as he plays the images in his mind of the montage created in the previous exercise: the Sousa trumpet, the wiping of the eyes, digging his own grave with his bare hands, howling a rage against fate, embracing the shepherd, a happy tap dance to obliterate his misery, a frenzied search for a blade to amputate his hand, and so on.

He keeps doing it until the potential for mental chaos is linked to the gesture found earlier.

8. Motivate the beat with the gesture and the key phrase together.

The actor cues the beat by thinking *...the blood...STOP!...* as he makes the gesture of Oedipus glancing at his palm. He repeats this until thought and deed, one after the other in a flash of instinct, become second nature. The result is a double gesture—hands reading for the shepherd's throat stopped suddenly by the gestures of the upturned palm—that is in effect a single action of thought and deed informed by the character's mental chaos.

Having successfully embodied the risk that anything could happen, the actor playing the legendary Oedipus has earned the right to play his unique version of Oedipus's ageless choice to blind himself as if it has never been played before.

Equally important, the combined exercises have created an instinctive habit in the actor/character that all his choices are up for grabs; a heightened sense of readiness that keeps an audience in suspense from Oedipus's entrance to the extraordinary act of gouging out his own eyes at the climax of the play.

Our final three exercises are designed to shape a performance and give it a sense of being an aesthetic whole. Let's take another look at the actor playing Masha. She, along with all the other actors we've seen, has done all the work to make herself ready for performance. She is ready to add the final touches.

12.
Shaping Performance

Context

By this time, the work of characterization has been largely accomplished. The coming three exercises are intended to complete the integration of interpretation and character behavior by adding moments of emphasis, subtle subtextual nuances, and, in some of the critical moments, more overt behavior. It's time now to go public: to shape the feelings, words, movements, and gestures of the character into an integrated whole.

While it's understood that the shape of a production is first envisioned by the playwright in collaboration with producer, director, and designers, their artistry alone cannot fully express the aesthetic beauty of the dramatic form without the shapes of the actors' performances. An actor's performance is not only the revelation of character, it's an artistic whole with an aesthetic beauty of its own embedded within the narrative shape of the play—a wholeness seen and heard by the audience as a live-action moving portrait of character.

Structure and rhythmic energy

A play is a vehicle for integrating the aesthetic whole of an actor's performance into the aesthetic whole of a production. The playwright's intention, spoken or not, is *de facto* yet another version of the universal struggle between self and fate. In this light, imagine a play as the vehicle to drive its passengers to an unknown but predetermined fate, and the assembled parts of the play's structure provide the rhythmic energy that fuels a character's journey to its destination.

Think of the characters in *Three Sisters* as passengers in the vehicle of the play: some of them are going along for the ride (Natasha, who wants to rise in class and attain wealth); some of them want a similar destination (all three sisters, who want to return to a better life as they knew it in Moscow); some are detoured by events (Masha, by her affair with Vershinin).

Consider how the different needs and objectives of the characters set them not only in conflict with one another but also with the vehicle of the play, which is trying to keep them on the road to a predetermined fate. These conflicts are reflected in the rhythm and tempo of the journey—rhythm being the pattern of the beats within the structure of the play and tempo the speed at which the beats are played.

As noted, a beat is marked by a *recognizable change in thought and/or feeling*. For our purposes in the next exercises, a beat in a scene can be an *action beat*, where character intention affects plot behavior directly (most often as movement), or an *internal beat*, where a change of thought alone causes a change in the character's inner life. (This internal moment of change will later affect external behavior—usually as gesture.)

Think of the action beats as the rhythm of the play— that is, the movement of the plot—and the internal beats as the tempo of the character's behavior within the rhythm of the plot. In performance, play and character working together create the rhythmic energy of the aesthetic whole. Let's have a look at how a play is structured to clarify how action beats and internal beats are used.

There are four primary elements that constitute the main structural frame of a play: exposition, crisis, climax, and denouement. Exposition starts the play and drives it to a crisis. A crisis drives the play to a climax that resolves the crisis. The denouement is the arrival of the play at its destination. The exposition, crisis, climax, and denouement serve as the primary action beats that establish the rhythm of the play.

The additional structures that support the main frame are acts, composed of scenes, which are usually definitively noted. There are smaller unannounced scenes within scenes, often called "French scenes," usually marked by the entrance or exit of another character. For example, in *Three Sisters*, Natasha's crossing through the room in Act III marks the start of the "French scene" that contains Masha's confession. Andrey's entrance starts a new scene within the larger scene of the act.

The structure of each scene replicates that of the main frame, with one exception. Plays have denouements but acts and scenes do not: scenes lead to more scenes. So, their structure is most times made of three action beats only: exposition, crisis, and the climax that resolves the crisis. (Some scenes may use false denouements to affect plot. For our purposes, we'll not use them here.)

Like the actor playing Oedipus, the actor playing Masha has done the work of earning her choices. Now, she revisits the confession in Act III to create a moving portrait of Masha.

Imagine behavior as a series of individual still moments bound together in a picture book of the play. Now imagine running the pages quickly, one after the other, with your thumb, the way kids used to do with those little books that make action cartoons. Just so, we can think of behavior on stage as a series of still life portraits that create a moving picture of character.

In the first of the three following exercises, the actor will establish a pattern of Masha's external behavior from some of the habitual gestures and movements Masha has already expressed in rehearsals. In the second exercise, she will create a template of three still life portraits for the three action beats—exposition, crisis, and climax—that move the scene. Then she will commit the portraits to muscle memory. In the third exercise, she will combine the habitual behavior she realized in the first exercise with the template of the three still lifes she created in the second to complete a moving portrait of Masha's external behavior.

To prepare for the exercises, the actor playing Masha makes note of what happens in each of the three action beats:

- The *expository beat* happens at the beginning of the scene when Masha sits up in response to Natasha who has just walked through their private space.
- The *crisis beat* happens as Masha moves and confesses, "I love, I love…I love that man…"
- The *climactic beat* happens at the very end of the confession when Masha says, "…silence…"

The actor playing Masha will find experiences from movements and gestures for the expository, crisis, and climactic beats that serve the plot. She will use variations of the exercises to create a body within a body and commit the feeling life from those experiences to body memory as habits of behavior.

An Exercise to Establish a Feeling Basis for Habits of Behavior

1. Find possible habits.

The actor has been playing Masha as a woman whose passion and intelligence find refuge from boredom and frustration in her affair with Vershinin: a woman whose conflicted behavior can be described as both young and old, full of despair and clinging to hope, bitterly ironic and moved by music, short-tempered and longing for love.

Looking back at her rehearsals, she will find a few movements and gestures she made which are good candidates to become habitual behavior. She finds five to incorporate into Masha's behavior in the real time of the confession scene.

(1.) When Masha wants to avoid unpleasantness, she makes *a subtle shooing motion with her left hand,* as if to push it behind her—for example, when she starts to leave Irina's party early in Act I.

(2.) She *fiddles with her brooch* when she is made nervous by her attraction to Vershinin.

(3.) She *rubs her brow* when her husband's neediness threatens to give her a headache.

(4.) She *lightly lays the palm of one hand on the back of her other hand* as Vershinin had put his hand on hers when they were first introduced.

(5.) She *puts her left thumb on her right wrist to feel her pulse* whenever she needs proof of her own existence.

The next two steps will provide a feeling basis for expressing the gestures.

2. Breathe in the character's life passion of suffering.

The actor breathes in the life passion of Masha's suffering, which she first experienced as the image of Masha's father's coffin under a lone oak by the seashore at the opening of Act I.

3. Connect the life suffering to the key phrase in the working scene.

The actor has earlier chosen "my soul is aching" as the key phrase that most expresses Masha's life suffering, the feeling that motivates Masha's need to confess.

First, she breathes in the feeling life of the mantra "my soul is aching." Then, while in the feeling inspired by "my soul is aching," the actor calls up the mandala (image) of coffin, oak, and seashore. From that image, she breathes in the feeling of her life's suffering until it blends with the feeling from "my soul is aching. The life suffering and present suffering are now the one essential feeling source for Masha's external behavior in the confession scene.

In the following exercise, the actor playing Masha will create still life portraits for the action beats of the play. For clarity, I will title each portrait and use a fresh set of numbers for the steps in each one. The exercises are meant as a continuous sequence. The portraits, when taken together in sequence, make a visual synopsis of the story of Masha's journey through the play.

An Exercise to Create a Template of Still Life Portraits

Part One: A Portrait for the Expository Beat

1. Find a like experience elsewhere in the play for use in the current scene.

The three sisters are in Olga and Irina's bedroom. Two beds separated by a screen for privacy from a sitting area. A divan upon which Masha is resting. The *expository* beat occurs when Natasha enters through one door on one side of the room, walks across the stage, exits through the door on the other side.

The first of the like experiences the actor finds elsewhere in the play seems particularly appropriate to best express a feeling portrait of Masha's temper for the expository beat. In Act II, almost immediately after Vershinin has declared his love for Masha, he is called away by the latest of his wife's supposed attempts to kill herself. Masha explodes in a fit of mindless, frustrated anger, then sits in a huff. Natasha, symbol of the misery of the sisters' lives, in all her pretentious sincerity admonishes Masha (in badly accented French) to not be so vulgar.

2. Breathe in the feeling from the earlier like experience.

The actor breathes in the feeling of anger at Natasha's pretentious, badly accented sincerity.

3. Create a portrait for the expository beat.

Masha is lying on the divan in the confession scene. As Natasha enters, she becomes angry, as she did earlier in the play when Natasha admonished her with that cooing sincerity of hers. Natasha now walks, uninvited, through the sisters' private space. As soon as she exits, Masha sits up, feet planted like a duck, legs spread apart, hands flat on thighs, face jutted forward, twisted in pugnacious anger. The actor has found the still life portrait for the expository beat.

4. Repeat.

The actor playing Masha repeats lying on the divan, getting angry, and sitting up in a huff until the still life portrait of the expository beat is committed to muscle memory.

5. Speak the expository beat.

The actor remains in the sitting portrait as she speaks all of Masha's dialogue in the expository beat up to the moment for the crisis beat.

6. Repeat.

She repeats the process as many times as it takes for her muscle memory to mold itself to the spoken life of the beat from the sit to the crisis beat.

Part Two: A Portrait for the Crisis Beat

1. Find a like experience elsewhere in the play for the crisis beat in the current scene.

The crisis beat happens when Masha decides to ease the aching in her soul by confessing her love for Vershinin to her sisters. The actor finds a like experience in Act II when Vershinin kisses her hand and declares his love. Masha's response is an eager anticipation for something she dares not comprehend. It's too good to be true. And too thrilling to ignore. Not knowing how to respond, she hums a tune and dances to it for a moment or two, which ends with a portrait of Masha, her hands behind her head, looking at an imagined sky, exulting in a glimpse of freedom from her miserable world.

2. Breathe in the feeling from the earlier like experience.

The actor breathes in the exultation from Act II.

3. Create a portrait for the crisis beat.

From the feeling of exultation in the earlier like experience, Masha decides, in the confession scene, to respond to her sisters' unwillingness to hear her confession by creating a still life dance portrait, hands behind her head, looking exultantly at an imagined sky, to convince her sisters of her love for Vershinin. The actor has found the still life portrait for the crisis beat.

4. Repeat.

The actor repeats the feeling of exultation at Vershinin's declaration of love that produces the gesture of Masha's hands behind her head as she looks up at the sky, until the still life portrait and the crisis beat are married.

5. Speak the crisis beat.

The actor remains in the still life portrait as she speaks all of Masha's dialogue from the beginning of the crisis beat up to the moment of the climactic beat.

6. Repeat.

She repeats the process as many times as it takes for her muscle memory to mold the still life portrait of hands behind her head, looking at thy sky, in the crisis moment.

Now she adds a next step.

7. Speak all the dialogue of the two still life portraits in succession.

Next, the actor speaks the dialogue of the expository beat while remaining in its still life portrait (the sit), then immediately moves into the dance still life portrait (hands behind her head, looking at the sky) as she speaks the dialogue of the crisis beat.

8. Repeat the process.

She repeats the process as many times as it takes for her muscle memory to give the actor a sense of how one portrait evolves into another.

Part Three: A Portrait for the Climactic Beat

1. Find a like experience for the climactic beat.

The climactic beat of the confession scene ends with Masha's reference to Gogol's *Diary of a Madman* in the last sentence of the scene: "I'll be like Gogol's madman…silence…silence…." In her search for where in rehearsals she might find a portrait for the climactic beat, the actor remembers a moment at the beginning of the play when Masha was reading Pushkin. The actor realizes Masha was feeling forever confined to the misery of her life. And now, as she feels it again, she flashes a portrait of Masha in a straitjacket. This is the portrait she will use for the climactic beat.

2. Breathe in the feeling from the earlier like experience.

She breathes in the feeling of confinement Masha gets from reading Pushkin, as he reminds her of the limitations of her life.

3. Create a portrait of the climactic beat.

The actor breathes in the feeling of confinement and hugs herself as if in a straitjacket to create a still life portrait for the climactic beat.

4. Repeat.

Repeat until the feeling of confinement and the still life portrait of Masha hugging herself are married.

5. Speak the dialogue of the climactic beat.

She speaks all the dialogue of the climactic beat as she remains in the still life of hugging herself.

6. Repeat.

She repeats the process as many times as it takes for her muscle memory to mold the spoken dialogue to the still life of hugging herself from the end of the crisis beat of looking up at the sky to the end of the climactic beat.

7. Speak the dialogue of all three still life portraits in succession.

The actor speaks all the dialogue of each of the three still life portraits in succession. She makes and holds the portrait (the sit) as she speaks the dialogue of the expository beat. Then she makes and holds the portrait (looking at the sky) as she speaks the dialogue of the crisis. She does the same with the hugging portrait of the climactic beat.

8. Repeat.

Repeat until body memory can change portraits and speak the dialogue of each beat in succession with ease.

From her work with the first two exercises the actor has created a template of muscle memory that will serve as an intuitive basis for a visual, in-motion portrait of Masha's external behavior in the play. The final exercise will make those motion pictures of Masha's life spontaneous realities.

An Exercise to Create a Moving Portrait of Character

1. Reconnect to each of the three portraits.

Without speaking the words, the actor playing Masha works the portrait of the sit in the anger of the expository beat: feeling-portrait, feeling-portrait, etcetera, until she's satisfied the connection is still solid.

She repeats the process with the crisis portrait and the climactic portrait. When satisfied, she's ready for step 2.

2. Run the three portraits as a live moving portrait throughout the play.

The actor runs the portraits, one after the other with feeling but no dialogue, and with no break in between them. Her purpose is to set the sequence as a continuing presence in Masha's body memory that will instinctively behave as the source for all the variations of Masha's external behavior throughout the play.

3. Integrate all the work into the scene.

The actor now works the confession scene in its entirety, words and all. At this point, the portraits are ready to provide the subtextual source for the expository, crisis, and climactic beats as well as the habitual internal character beats.

In the example below, the three portraits are in bold; habitual behavior is italicized in parentheses. Other stage directions are unitalicized.

The scene begins in response to Natasha's crossing through the room.

The Moving Portrait

Masha: (**sits up,** *rises, uses the shooing hand gesture as she walks toward the door where Natasha left.*) She walks as if she's the one who set the town on fire.

Olga: Masha, you're silly, you're the silliest of the family. Please forgive me for saying so. (Pause)

Masha: I want to make a confession, dear sisters. Yes, my soul is aching. I'll confess to you and never again to anyone…I'll tell you this minute. (softly, fiddles with her brooch) It's my secret but you must know everything…I can't be silent… **(pause, she holds her hands behind her head, looking up to an imagined sky in exultation.)** I love, I love…I love that man…You just now saw him…Why don't I say it…Yes, I'll say it… I love Vershinin.

Olga: (goes out of sight behind the screen, leaving Masha with Irina) Stop that. I'm not listening to you.

Masha: (calling after Olga) But what can I do? (*rubs her brow*) [3] At first, he seemed odd to me, then I was sorry for him…then I fell in love with him (*caresses the back of her right hand softly with her left hand*) …fell in love with his voice, his words, his misfortunes, his two daughters.

Olga: (Behind the screen) I'm not listening. Talk any nonsense you like, I won't listen

Masha: Oh, Olga, you are foolish, I love him. But what can I do? (*fiddles with her brooch again*) I love him…It is my fate…It's my lot…And he loves me…It's all so terrible, so awful …. But can it be so wrong?… (*Masha puts her left thumb on her right wrist to feel her pulse,* then takes Irina by the hand and draws her to her bosom) Oh, my dear…How are we going to live our lives, what is to become of us? When you read a novel it all seems so old and simple, but when you fall in love yourself, then you learn that nobody knows anything, and everyone must decide for themselves…My dear ones, my sisters…I have made my confession to you, and now I'll be silent…. Like Gogol's madman, I'll be silent… **(she wraps her arms around herself as in a straitjacket, eyes in a catatonic blank, and softly utters the last:)** silence…

The actor playing Masha has put the last touches on her work by giving shape to her performance. She has committed to muscle memory three still life portraits of Masha. Each portrait is now a bedrock of muscular activities that contain the instinctive impulses that, in concert with all the work she has done on the character's inner life, serves as a template from which to tell the story of Masha's journey in the play, in word and deed.

She's ready to go public with a live moving portrait of Masha that will play with the pleasing aesthetic of a consistent and spontaneous whole from the moment we first see her reading Pushkin to the final fade of light as she watches Vershinin leave with his troops.

The Wrap

Just as the actor playing Masha offers her own passion for life in a particular way to experience Chekov's tragicomic mix of joy, yearning, sorrow, and happiness, all the actors who have graced the pages of this book have made their own specific contributions to the view of life expressed in their respective productions.

It's quite an accomplishment for an actor to start from a moment of inspiration and arrive at a finely detailed, spontaneous performance of a character's life that is unique to the actor's own special gifts—a performance that, in collaboration with the production, makes a distinctive contribution to the playgoer's view of life.

Consider the devotion required of an actor to create such a character, crafted from the challenge implicit in the long sentence with nine commas we first saw in Chapter 6 that signifies the task of creating a character: every feeling moment on stage is made up of passion, thought process, and emotional behavior, happening simultaneously in past, present, and future in some combination of actor and character, in a certain place that contains certain objects, under certain conditions, at a certain historical moment, within the circumstances of a given culture.

Hopefully, no later than two weeks before the first audition, and probably through at least two callbacks, the actor has worked at home and continued working from first rehearsal on. They have done the work required to marry the passion of their life to the character's by sharing their mental, psychic, and spiritual feelings, and used their physical and vocal skills to shape a spontaneous performance expressed with a simple, economic, revealing aesthetic unmistakably their own.

The actor continues to work from opening night all the way to closing, perfecting a detail here and there, to keep themself available to all the nuances of behavior that happen in the newness from one performance to the next—a performance that expands the view of life for actor and audience alike. Neither production nor audience need ask any less of an actor.

> Lights down, curtain closed.
> Curtain open, lights up.
> It's time for a company call.

The applause actors receive during curtain call is something more than a simple thank you to the actors. It's also a celebration of their individual artistry for the seeming extraordinary accomplishment of actors to become something more of themselves by becoming somebody else. Actor and audience alike share the ontological passion for survival this book is based on. A passion that is, by instinct, home to a seed of universal hope that we might possibly have a say in our own destiny. A passion that, when shared, releases actor and audience alike from the boundaries of self into the larger comprehension of being *us*.

Paul Austin has been an actor, director, and teacher for all his professional life in the theatre. He has acted and directed On and Off Broadway, Off-Off Broadway, in summer stock and regional theatres around the nation, as well as acting for television and film. Recent stage appearances include the title role in *Krapp's Last Tape,* Foreman in Vaclav Havel's *Audience.* and Niels Bohr in *Copenhagen.* He has directed over 50 plays. In addition to his working life as actor and director, he has founded and been Artistic Director of three theatres: the Image Theatre in Boston, the Image Theatre and Studio on Theatre Row in Manhattan, and the Liberty Free Theatre, free for an underserved community in upstate New York. He has been a member of the Ensemble Studio Theatre since its founding. All through his career, he has taught acting at his own studios and as a guest at various institutions. He was tenured acting and directing faculty at Sarah Lawrence College for eighteen years. Hundreds of actors who've worked with him have had continuing careers in the theatre. Mr. Austin was a recipient of the Teachers who Make a Difference award from the Creative Coalition at the Sundance Film Festival in 2013.